MARRIAGE
IS LOVE FOREVER

REV. JAMES SOCIAS, J.C.D.

MARRIAGE
IS LOVE FOREVER

Adapted to the Catechism of the Catholic Church

Scepter Publishers
Midwest Theological Forum

A number of friends and colleagues read all or part of the manu-
script and provided helpful comments and criticisms.
I wish in particular to thank Carman Fallace, Jim and Joyce Coughlin,
Dick and Lou Prince and Fr. Joseph Penna.
I am also grateful to John Powers for his interest in the book and to
Fr. Mubarak Anwar Amar for his careful editing of the manuscript.

Published by

Scepter Publishers
20 Nassau St.
Princeton, NJ 08542
Tel. (800) 322-8773

Midwest Theological Forum
1410 W. Lexington St.
Chicago, IL 60607
Tel. (312) 421-8129

Nihil Obstat: Msgr. William B. Smith, STD
Censor Librorum
May 7, 1994

Imprimatur: ✠ Patrick Sheridan, DD,
Vicar General, Archdiocese of New York
May 7, 1994

Excerpts from the English translation of the *Catechism of the Catholic Church* ©
1994, United States Catholic Conference, Inc.—Libreria Editrice Vaticana. Excerpts from the English translation of the *Rite of Marriage* © 1969, International
Committee on English in the Liturgy, Inc. (ICEL); Excerpts from the English translation of *The Roman Missal* © 1973, ICEL. All rights reserved.

Scripture readings of the Wedding Mass are taken from *The Jerusalem Bible* © 1966
Darton, Longman & Todd, Ltd. and Doubleday, a division of Bantam Doubleday
Dell Publishing Group Inc.

Printed in the United States of America
Second Edition, 1994

ISBN 0-933932-53-7

CONTENTS

FOREWORD

By

His Eminence John Cardinal O'Connor
Archbishop of New York

My parents, mother and father alike, might shudder to know that I frequently reflect on their marriage as I work with engaged couples preparing for the Sacrament of Marriage. Theirs was as real a marriage as I have ever known— not perfect, but very real. That is why I think they might shudder to know that I still regard their marriage so highly, because it wasn't perfect. There were pain and illness and misunderstandings and even periods of alienation. There were hurt and anger and conflict and the everyday struggles of raising a family during difficult times. But above all there was faith in God and, grounded in that faith, there was an unalterable commitment of husband and wife. For my parents, marriage was indeed a Sacrament.

These are no less difficult days for engaged and married couples. Preparation for marriage often seems to consist largely in selecting reception halls and attendants' wardrobes The menu and wedding band are chosen only after careful thought and comparison shopping. Following an engagement there may be little time for the man and woman to prepare themselves spiritually and emotionally for the radical and remarkable event about to occur. Once married, a couple is confronted with a barrage of media reports about celebrity divorces, remarriages or "arrangements". Even more frequently, the very concept of marriage is ridiculed as antiquated, and some now suggest that marriage is belittling to women.

Difficult as it may be in today's culture, however. marriage continues to be the fundamental relationship in our society. Twenty-five years ago, Pope Paul VI in his encyclical, *Humanæ Vitæ*, affirmed the Catholic Church's belief in the sanctity of marriage in the modern world. He set the context in which we might better understand and appreciate the love that exists between husband and wife, and he defended the truth and dignity of conjugal love and family love in the light of God's plan. He spoke of marriage as "the wise institution of the Creator to realize in humanity his design of love." In our own days Pope John Paul II has repeatedly stressed the importance of marriage for family life and the stability of society.

In *Marriage is Love Forever*, Father James Socias presents in very readable form the teaching of the Church on the Sacrament of Marriage. Within the context of this teaching, Father Socias gives very practical advice for engaged and married couples about ways they can deepen their understanding of marriage and their commitment to it. This book should be beneficial to all those who are preparing or who wish to prepare others for the Sacrament of Marriage according to the authentic teaching of the Catholic Church. May it get widespread attention and use so that the marriages of the future may be blessed with unwavering faith and unconditional love.

New York
June 21, 1994

PREFACE

Our culture has over-romanticized sex and, in the process, has made it synonymous with love, at least in the popular mind. The over-riding message of movies, books and the whole culture is that if a young person finds the right partner, violins will play, fireworks will go off, and life will become perfect. If the popular culture of the last quarter-century and more is to be believed, all one needs to find happiness is to discover Mr. or Ms. Right and enter a meaningful relationship with that person.

But the unhappiness and frustration evident in so many romantic relationships from the teenagers' first date to the young adults' trial marriage, tells another story. Somewhere along the way, our culture's view of romance went awry. Instead of life-long happiness, all many people have to show for their last relationship is a certificate of divorce and a wounded soul. Many who have been through the sad experience of divorce or separation may have avoided such wounds if they had been taught about the profound spiritual nature of our sexuality and its relationship to the vocation of marriage.

Is there another way? Can marital love bring happiness in today's world? If we realize the true meaning of marriage, then the answer is an emphatic "yes." If love between a man and a woman is actually to mean something, it must be founded upon more than the electricity that sparks in their eyes when they first meet although this too has a purpose in God's plan. Real love must differ somehow from the typical relationship of today as it is portrayed in the media.

Even the most cynical sexual revolutionaries sometimes speak in whispers of life-long relationships that bring happiness. Although they scoff at the view that marriage must be a permanent commitment to bring fulfillment, they admit that happiness can come from a life-long marriage. But they fail to realize that without a life-long commitment, relationships will quickly become empty, selfish exercises in self-gratification which soon bring unhappiness. When we consider that a good marriage is much more vital to personal happiness than career or business success, it becomes even more clear that most of us spend an inadequate amount of time preparing for it.

For those who recognize that love without a life-long commitment ends in failure, Christ and his Church can show the way to the true meaning of love. In the midst of a culture that relentlessly misinforms and misleads on the subject, the Church proclaims the 'good news' regarding sexuality and offers couples the hope that fidelity, virtue and thus peace and joy are attainable. To say that one wishes to marry someone for life is certainly a difficult proposition—one not to be treated lightly.

If love and sex are not the same thing, there must be a reason for sex within the context of love. Sex is for conjugal union and procreation, between husband and wife who wish to perpetuate their love in a new life. Both aspects, unitive and procreative, are designed by God to enable spouses to grow in holiness.

Love, if it is to be life-long, must be based on an understanding of one's beloved, rather than a simple sexual attraction. It must want to give to the other, rather than use the other for self-satisfaction. It must also be open to bringing new children of God into the world. But love of one's spouse and one's children alone is still not enough to get us to the final point. Something is needed to help those who wish to marry in their struggle to remain together. That aid is the sacrament of marriage itself.

Through the sacrament of marriage, and through proper preparation for marriage, those Christians who wish to be faithful to one another will always receive the grace necessary to fulfill their marital vocation. They will learn to love each other better by loving God. They will realize that their marriage is not a simple contract between two people, but a sacred covenant which has received its special nature from Christ himself. Because of this sacramental status, and because of the nature of conjugal love itself, marriage is indissoluble. But the very nature of the sacrament also provides those who receive it with all the grace necessary to follow the Church's teachings regarding it. Among these is the grace to go through married life united with Christ.

Loving someone for one's entire life, after all, is difficult. The cynics of today will tell you that often. But instead of providing help to live out a commitment, they champion the expedient answer, that of divorce, as liberating. But that way leads only to unhappiness, for both the parents and the children. The way of Christian marriage may be more difficult, but it offers the vital help of grace to accomplish this task and gives the only true promise of real happiness in love.

This book is a short but thorough treatment of the most common concerns and questions regarding Catholic marriage for pastors and couples alike. To the uninitiated, some of the guidelines prescribed may seem too demanding. To those of you who have been initiated, the same prescriptions and proscriptions may ring truer as the years pass.

Furthermore, it is an explanation of the Catholic Church's teachings on the dignity and sanctity of marriage, how best to prepare for marriage, the nature of the sacrament of marriage, and the material arrangements for the ceremony. It is hoped that those preparing for marriage and priests helping to prepare others for marriage will find this work beneficial.

Rev. James P. Socías

ABBREVIATIONS USED
IN FOOTNOTES

In citing works in the notes, short titles have generally been used.
Works frequently cited have been identified by the following abbreviations.

C. C. C.	*Catechism of the Catholic Church.* Rome, Libreria Editrice Vaticana, 1992.
C. I. C.	*Codex Iuris Canonici (Code of Canon Law).* Rome, Libreria Editrice Vaticana, 1983.
D. E.	*Directory for Ecumenism.* National Conference of Catholic Bishops (N.C.C.B.). Origins vol 23, no. 9, July 29, 1993.
F. C.	*Familiaris Consortio: The Role of the Family in the Modern World.* John Paul II. Rome, Libreria Editrice Vaticana, 1981.
F. W. L.	*Follow the Way of Love: Pastoral Message to Families.* N.C.C.B. Origins vol. 23 no. 25., 1993.
G. S.	*Gaudium et Spes.* Second Vatican Council. Rome, Libreria Editrice Vaticana,1965.
G. E.	*Gravissimum Educationis.* Second Vatican Council. Rome, Libreria Editrice Vaticana,1965.
H.V.	*Humanae Vitae.* Paul VI. Rome, Libreria Editrice Vaticana, 1968.
L. F.	*Letter to Families.* John Paul II. Rome, Libreria Editrice Vaticana, 1994.
L. G.	*Lumen Gentium.* Second Vatican Council. Rome, Libreria Editrice Vaticana, 1964.
M. D.	*Mulieris Dignitatis.* John Paul II. Rome, Libreria Editrice Vaticana, 1988.
N. C. C. B.	National Conference of Catholic Bishops of the United States.
O. C. J.	*One in Christ Jesus: Toward a Pastoral Response to the Concerns of Women for Church and Society.* N.C.C.B. *Ad Hoc Committee* for a Pastoral Response to Women's Concerns, Origins Vol. 22; no. 29, 1993.
S. C.	*Sacrosanctum Concilium.* Second Vatican Council. Rome, Libreria Editrice Vaticana, 1963.

PART I

INTRODUCTION

INTRODUCTION

For a Christian, marriage is not just a social institution, much less a mere remedy for human weakness. It is a real supernatural calling. *A great sacrament, in Christ and in the Church,* says St. Paul.[1] At the same time, it is a permanent contract between a man and a woman.

Most Christians have a vocation to marriage. As a vocation, marriage was established by God and has been continuously blessed by him since the time of our first parents.

Of all the possibilities in creation, God chose to make us male and female. God saw that it was not good for man to be alone and created a partner for him.[2] It was in God's plan that each provide companionship for the other, seeking the good of the spouse. In paradise, God established the bond of marriage. From the beginning, marriage was considered a sacred union between husband and wife. It remained as such until the coming of Christ, who raised this bond to the sacrament of Matrimony. Christian marriage then becomes a sign of the covenant between Christ and his Church. *Since it signifies and communicates grace, marriage between baptized persons is a true sacrament of the New Covenant.*[3] Just as Christ is inseparable from the Church, the sacrament of marriage, entered freely, creates an inviolable bond between husband and wife.

In this unbreakable bond of marriage, husband and wife are joined together, united with Christ, becoming one flesh and perfecting human love. Husband and wife receive the strength of the sacramental graces necessary to fulfill their

---

1. Cf. *Ephesians* 5:32.
2. Cf. *Genesis* 2:18.
3. C.C.C. 1617.

marital duties. This inner strength is necessary in all family life, especially at its critical moments when the love which was expressed in the liturgical rite of marital consent with the words: *I promise to be faithful to you always . . . all the days of my life,* is put to a difficult test.

Only persons are capable of saying those words; only they are able to live in communion on the basis of a mutual choice which is, or ought to be, fully conscious and free. The Book of Genesis, in speaking of a man who leaves father and mother in order to cleave to his wife, highlights the conscious and free choice which gives rise to marriage, making the son of a family a husband, and the daughter of a family a wife.

When they are united by the conjugal covenant in such a way as to become *one flesh*, their union ought to take place in truth and love, and thus express the maturity proper to persons created in the image and likeness of God.[4]

Because marriage is the image of the union between God and his Church, Christ is its model. Nevertheless, in today's society, we are constantly bombarded with false images of marriage. Romantic books, movies, soap operas and numerous other sources create a sensational propaganda of sexual passion that has little or nothing to do with the Christian concept of love and marriage.

The real meaning of the sacrament can only be given by Jesus Christ through his Church. That is why a man and a woman planning for marriage need to spend time in reflection and preparation. This preparation requires an adequate probe into the meaning of love and into God's plan for married life. It involves several steps prior to the wedding ceremony, and the acquisition of good habits throughout one's entire life.

Our first preparation for marriage—called remote preparation—starts in early childhood when we begin to acquire

4. Cf. L.F. 7-8.

the essential values of human life and the basic development of the human virtues. From our parents, family, and teachers, we receive a sound spiritual and catechetical formation. This education continues into early adulthood, when we begin taking more concrete steps toward our life as adults in society.

Proximate preparation involves a more specific preparation for the sacrament. It is in this period that we acquire our religious formation, and study marriage in more depth.

Through our religious education we begin to learn what to look for in a future spouse. This stage also demands a certain "settling down" in a career or job so as to be able to provide adequately for a family.

Finally, the immediate preparation takes place in the months and weeks before the wedding ceremony. It involves an intense and in-depth study of the meaning of marriage. It also requires practical preparations for the wedding ceremony and the first few weeks after marriage. Today, emphasis is often on such practical preparations leaving couples unprepared for the spiritual journey of marriage.

Much of the success of a marriage depends on the adequate preparation of the future spouses. It is important to acquire a knowledge of certain elements of marriage that builds on a well-balanced understanding and spiritual formation acquired years before the wedding ceremony. In a society where many marriages fail, this preparation is crucial for a happy and lifelong marriage.[5] When we consider the efforts we put into preparation for career or business opportunities, the effort put into the marriage commitment is put into perspective.

5. Cf. C.C.C. 1632 and F.C. 23.

PART II

THE SACRAMENT OF MATRIMONY

A. GOD INSTITUTED MARRIAGE

Have you not read that from the beginning the Creator 'made them male and female' and said, 'For this reason a man shall leave his father and mother and be joined to his wife, and the two shall become one flesh'? So they are no longer two, but one flesh. Therefore, what God has joined together, no human being must separate.[6]

1. What is marriage? Where does it come from?

Marriage is a covenant between two persons, a man and a woman, who freely accept each other as partners in a mutual self-giving in the service of life. God established marriage as the ordinary vocation in life for most people, and Christ Himself raised marriage to a new and supernatural state by establishing the sacrament of Matrimony.

Christian Matrimony is the sacrament by which a man and a woman enter a holy covenant. Since Christ instituted this sacrament, he also gives a man and woman their vocation to marriage. The covenant thus involves not only a man and woman, but also Christ.

Just as those called to the priesthood or to a religious vocation spend a long time in prayer and preparation, those called to marriage should also spend time in prayer, preparing themselves to receive this sacrament.

By realizing that marriage is a vocation to holiness to which Christ calls us, and by seeking to be faithful to this call, we can find the key to a successful marriage. In the bond of marriage, Christ gives the husband and wife the sacramental grace necessary for the fulfillment of their marital duties.[7]

---

6. *Matthew 19:4-6.*

7. Cf. *Matthew 19:11.*

By coming to restore the initial order of creation disturbed by sin, Jesus himself has given people the strength and grace to live out their marriages in the new dimension of God's kingdom. By following Christ, denying themselves, and taking up their crosses, spouses will be able with Christ's help to accept[8] and live out *the original meaning of marriage.*[9]

In establishing marriage as a vocation in life, God gave it the characteristics that enable human love to achieve its perfection, and allow family life to be full and fruitful. *By its very nature*, the partnership that is established *is ordered to the good of the couple, as well as to the generation and education of children.*[10] Outside marriage, or without a proper realization of its nature, the right conditions for the fruitfulness of human love and for a successful family life do not exist.

Marriage was not invented by man. God himself established it when, in the garden of Paradise, he created our first parents. From the beginning, marriage has been much more than a human institution. It is the wise institution of God to accomplish in mankind his design of love. *The intimate community of love and life which constitutes the married state has been established by the Creator and endowed by him with its own proper laws. . . . God himself is the author of marriage.*[11]

2.   What do we mean when we say that marriage was raised by Christ to a Sacrament?

For Christians, Christ raised this union of husband and wife to the dignity of a sacrament. It became a holy covenant, an *image of the union of Christ and his Church* and a source of special grace. St. Paul wrote: *Husbands, love your wives, just as Christ loved the Church and delivered himself up*

8. Cf. *Matthew 19:11.*

9. C.C.C. 1615.

10. Cf. C.I.C. 1055.1 and C.C.C. 1601, 1660.

11. G.S. 48; cf. C.C.C. 1603 and H.V. 8.

for her, that he might sanctify her. . . .[12] Our model for marriage cannot be based on images propagated by society, but on Christ, his Church, and the Holy Family.

The real meaning of the sacrament of marriage can only be given by Jesus Christ through the Church. Marriage requires a basic understanding of the Christian faith and the true nature of the sacrament of Matrimony. A marriage, validly contracted between baptized persons, is always a sacrament of Christ and his Church.[13] By virtue of the sacramentality of their marriage, (Christian) spouses are bound to one another in the most profound and indissoluble manner. Their belonging to each other is the real representation, by means of the sacramental sign, of the very relationship of Christ with the Church.[14]

---

12. *Ephesians* 5:25.

13. Cf. C.I.C. 1055.2 and C.C.C. 1617.

14. Cf. C.C.C. 1617 and F.C. 13.

B. LEARNING TO LOVE

*Be subordinate to one another out of reverence for
Christ . . . each one of you should love his wife as himself, and the wife should respect her husband.*[15]

3. What is conjugal love?

Our society often promotes the romantic idea of *love at
first sight*, in which a man and a woman know that they are
destined to spend their lives together. While God may give
a vocation to marriage in different ways, it is unwise to
decide on marriage *at first sight*. The couple should spend
time in getting to know each other before that decision is
finalized.

Love between future spouses begins while they are
dating, and this love stems from a gradual revelation of
oneself to the other. Little by little, mutual knowledge
grows, and from this knowledge grows love.

Knowledge and love reach a point of readiness for a
life-long commitment which culminates giving oneself en-
tirely and exclusively to the other in soul and body. This
time is when marriage, as the complete surrender of husband and wife to each other, according to the law of God,
becomes necessary. As Jesus told his disciples, *'Have you
not read that the Creator, from the beginning, made them male
and female, and said, 'for this reason a man shall leave his father
and his mother and cleave to his wife'.*[16]

*Conjugal love involves a totality, in which all the elements
of the person enter—appeal of the body and instinct, power of
feeling and affectivity, aspiration of spirit and of will. It aims at
a deeply personal unity, the unity that, beyond union in one flesh,
leads to forming one heart and soul; it demands indissolubility
and faithfulness in definitive mutual giving; and it is open to*

15. *Ephesians 5:21, 5:33.*

16. *Matthew 19:4-5.*

fertility. In a word, it is a question of the normal characteristics of all natural conjugal love; but with a new significance which not only purifies and strengthens them, but raises them to the extent of making them the expression of specifically Christian values.[17]

Authentic married love is caught up into divine love and directed and reached by the redemptive power of Christ and the salvific action of the Church.[18] The ideal marriage requires that kind of spousal love. Such genuine love should have certain qualities for it to be a reflection of the love of God, and not a mere passing passion. This spousal love should be:

- *Fully human*: it does not come only from the senses, but also primarily from the spirit. It includes a willingness to suffer for others, since *as long as we walk on this earth, suffering is the touchstone of love.*[19]
- *Total*: it leads the spouses to share *all* without unnecessary reservation or selfish calculations; a unique form of personal friendship where husband and wife generously share everything.
- *Faithful and exclusive:* in sickness and in health until death.
- *Fruitful:* it is extended in and through children, the *crown of Matrimony.*[20]

4. With whom can we fall in love? Why are there so many unhappy marriages?

Learning to love, truly falling in love with one's future spouse is a lesson to be learned before marriage. First, one

17. C.C.C. 1643 and F.C. 13.
18. Cf. C.C.C. 1639 and G.S. 48.
19. Josemaría Escrivá. *Christ is Passing By.* (Princeton, NJ: Scepter Publishers, Inc., 1975), 24.
20. Cf. C.C.C. 2373 and H.V. 9.

has to choose the right partner: otherwise the marriage will be a source of difficulties.

A good Christian should have the will power to avoid falling in love with:

- Those who are already engaged;
- Those who are already married;
- Those who are only physically attractive;
- Those who are impure or have lax moral standards;
- Those who are called by God to celibacy, *which demands one's whole heart and being.*[21]

Unhappy marriages often occur because there was inadequate preparation for choosing the right partner.

5.   Who educates for a Christian marriage?

Remote preparation for marriage is given by the parents. It should begin in early childhood, through wise family education and a good example that leads children to understand the correct concept of a Christian family.

The best lesson for a successful marriage that a child can receive is the good example of his own family. This early education becomes the solid foundation for future families. That gradual education of the young people, together with personal spiritual guidance, will develop especially the virtue of chastity and make them able to engage in an honorable marriage.

The role of pastors and the Christian community as the family of God is indispensable for the transmission of the human and Christian values of marriage and family.[22]

21. J. L. Soria. *On Purity.* (Princeton, NJ: Scepter Publishers, Inc., 1970).

22. C.C.C. 1632; cf. C.I.C. 1063.2 ; G.S. 49 and L.F. 16.

6.   Is *"going steady"* an important stage?

"Going steady" is an important stage. Future spouses, during that period, must discuss and agree on some guidelines. Otherwise, it is easy to be carried away by an emotional love without any direction. We Christians have God's law for our guide.

With a Christian outlook, *"going steady"* becomes:

- A *journey of hope* by which each learns to respect the other, a respect based on the fact that men and women are children of God and their bodies are temples of the Holy Spirit.

- A *school of love* whereby a man and a woman, while getting to know each other, also learn that self-sacrificing generosity with each other and with God is the main support of a happy marriage.

- An *apprenticeship in fidelity* that will enable them to persevere faithfully in their future marriage.[23]

Dating should be a time for growing in affection and for getting to know one another better. As in every school of love, it should be inspired not by a desire of receiving, but by a spirit of giving, understanding, respect, and gentle consideration.[24]

7.   What are some guidelines for courtship?

To prepare for a happy marriage:

- *Seek the company of wholesome persons* who share your Catholic faith and morals. In this atmosphere of wholesome friendship, you will likely meet your future spouse. Look for a person who is a Catholic in deed and in truth; who is serious about raising a good family and a Christian home; who is responsible and who values work; who is sincere and truthful; who is chaste and has a high regard for purity.

23. Cf. C.C.C. 2350.

24. Josemaría Escrivá. *Conversations.* (Princeton, NJ: Scepter Publishers, Inc., 1970), 97.

- *Start at the proper age.* There is a danger in entering serious relationships or engagement too soon. Relationships leading to marriage require maturity—a degree of mental and emotional development. Young men and women entering relationships too soon may not yet understand the dignity, beauty, seriousness and selflessness of marriage. Once dating has begun at the appropriate age, there is also a danger of continuing it for too long. Our cultural experience has been that early dating or *"going steady"* for too long invites temptation and is associated with premarital sexual involvement.

- *Seek the advice of your parents and your confessor or spiritual director.* They have the experience as well as the grace of state to see God's will in your life.

- *Study and understand the proper concept of marriage.* Be concerned about acquiring a well-formed conscience. Like other vocations and professions, marriage requires special knowledge. Ask your pastor for marriage instruction. Ask him for the right books and Church documents to read on the nature and purpose of marriage.

- *Get married not for your own happiness alone but for the happiness of your future spouse and children.* Genuine happiness comes to those who are generous. They are willing to give without expecting anything in return. They are ready to sacrifice themselves in everything for the persons they love and for whom they are responsible. Love means giving and sacrificing, without thinking about oneself or one's comfort first.

- *Have the right intention.* The purpose of marriage is also to create a Christian home, that is, to have children, to raise them in a Christian manner, and to lead them to heaven.

- *Keep in mind that a total union will only exist when you are validly married according to the laws of the Church.* Sexual relationships must be reserved for marriage. The proper conditions and graces for beginning a family are only present in marriage. Giving in to temptation before marriage indicates selfishness, which is a serious detriment to a future marriage. Moreover, giving in to temptation obscures the bond of unity that should come from the marital act. There is the danger that one may fall in love with sex and choose the wrong marriage partner.

- *Be understanding.* Put yourself in the shoes of your future spouse. Be positive and accommodating in your opinions.

- *Live a good Catholic life.* You need the grace of God as the foundation for your future marriage. Attend Mass and receive Holy Communion every Sunday and as often as possible. Go to Confession regularly. Observe the Commandments, particularly the sixth and the ninth, which safeguard purity.

- *Pray together for a holy and happy marriage.* Your life in the end will be weighed by God himself on how you have lived your married life. Consider marriage in the light of eternity and God's judgment, and ask for his help on entering this vocation. Entrust yourself particularly to the Blessed Virgin Mary and Saint Joseph, who formed the Holy Family with Jesus, our Saviour.

8.   What are the manifestations of love during courtship?

Courtship is the time to learn if a man and a woman are suited for marriage. Manifestations of love and affection during courtship are pure, sincere and joyful when there is mutual respect, understanding and self-denial. This does not mean there will not be tensions or disagreements. Indeed, the way these are resolved can indicate if the capacity to make sacrifices is present.

Love is shown essentially in the effort to deny oneself for the person loved. Asking for expressions of affection that belong to married love is always a selfish love that can never be sincere and joyful. In that case, the dignity of marriage will never be understood.[25]

9. What makes human love pure, sincere and cheerful?

Being pure during courtship gives joy, and provides the *test of character,* that is necessary for a happy marriage. Marriage is sacred; therefore, the preparation that precedes it should be pure.

Nothing that is opposed to the law of God can be natural. Whoever does not practice purity cannot properly develop love and respect, since the qualities of true love are rooted in a pure heart.

While still at that stage, a man and a woman should keep in mind God's design for the affection that draws them to each other. Dating cannot be just a romantic love adventure in which sexual purity is set aside. Chastity is a preparation for marriage because a man and a woman, trying to live purely, acquire a love that is pure, sincere and cheerful. It is a guarantee that the good of the other person is truly being sought.

When love is degraded, it becomes an impure sensual passion. It ceases to be love and becomes a selfish pleasure by which one person uses another. Such impure love obviously cannot be sincere and true.

10. Why is the practice of the virtue of chastity a joyful affirmation of our true love for God?

The practice of the virtue of chastity is a joyful affirmation of our true love for God because:

---

25. Cf. C.C.C. 2350.

- It is the most significant way of *giving glory to Him* in sharing his divine creative power according to His will.
- When we practice chastity we become more *an image and likeness of God.*[26]
- It allows us to feel the *fatherly hand of God* in our life.
- It is a sign of being *children of God.*
- It gives us the *freedom to serve others.*

Chastity means the successful integration of sexuality within the person and therefore his or her inner unity in body and soul. While sexuality clearly expresses our belonging to the bodily and biological world, it becomes personal and truly human only when integrated into the interpersonal relationship of man and woman, within the total and temporally unlimited gift of each to the other.

The virtue of chastity therefore involves the integrity of the person and the integrality of the gift.[27]

11. If true love is the gift of self, can we say that true love is primarily in the will? Is it not determined by feelings? Is love blind?

Some people say that being in love is all that matters and justifies everything. However, building love upon affections that cause one to violate the law of God endangers the very essence of any relationship.

What seems like love often falls short of the true meaning of love. Love is not merely a mutual and emotional attraction, nor only a product of our feelings. Love is more. Love is giving oneself personally and becoming spiritually one with the beloved. For this reason, one needs to use the will in order to love.

---

26. Cf. John Paul II. M.D. (Boston, MA: St. Paul Book and Media, 1988), 14.

27. C.C.C. 2337.

True love is shown in deeds and not only in affection, promises or sweet words. *Real human love* is based on the love of God that requires the desire to fulfill his Commandments.

How can this unselfish love grow and be the foundation for a future marriage? Of course, it cannot only be a product of one's emotions or feelings—so-called *blind love*, which is a blind impulse of passions. It has to be a tested and proven *spiritual love*, which requires a unity of minds.

Uncontrolled passionate feelings could easily lead to lust and impurity. Impurity never brings true happiness. It creates a sensual love that will look for additional sensual partners in the future. It debases the spiritual bond required in marriage and makes it a merely accidental coincidence of desires.

On the other hand, when love is rooted in reason, one learns how to accept and even love the defects of the future spouse, helping one's beloved to correct them. Unselfish love gives motives for unity that always outweigh any reasons for division.

12. Does love require sexual relationship before marriage?

There is a time and a place for everything. For sex, the time and place is within marriage, which gives grace to the spouses to love each other in Christian charity.

"Going steady" is the time for a gradual unveiling of one's real person to the other. Only within marriage does human sexuality achieve its full sense and perfection as a vehicle for a love that is mutual, exclusive, permanent and self-giving between a man and a woman. Sex cannot be a manifestation of love if it violates God's plan. Couples who approach the Church and request the sacrament of marriage are rejecting many of society's limited notions of sexuality.

When a society permits sexual behavior to be torn from its moorings in human love and marriage, when it treats sex as a mechanism for personal pleasure, it encourages a destructive mentality and diminishes the value of personal commitment and of human life itself.[28]

13. What is the plan of God for sex? What are the basic differences between sex and love?

The purpose of sex is procreation and the conjugal union between husband and wife. There is an inseparable connection, established by God, which man on his own initiative may not break, between the unifying and the procreative significance of the marriage act.

The marital act—at the same time—unites husband and wife in the closest intimacy, and together, makes them capable of generating new life. This union fosters the mutual self-giving of the spouses: by means of the reciprocal gift which is proper and exclusive to them, husband and wife tend toward that communion of their beings whereby they help each other toward personal perfection in order to collaborate with God in the begetting and rearing of new life.[29]

The Church teaches that these two aspects of marital intercourse—the strengthening of interpersonal unity between spouses and the procreation of the new life—are two inseparable goods. They are inseparable—not in the sense that both must be achieved in every act of conjugal intimacy, but in the sense that one may not deliberately act against either good in any marital act.[30]

For these reasons, separation of sex from marriage is one of the great contemporary sins. Sex without marriage goes against the plan God made from the beginning. Only

---

28. Committee for Pro-life Activities, N.C.C.B., July 25, 1993.

29. Cf. C.C.C. 2360-2363 and Paul VI. H.V. 15.

30. Cf. Committee for Pro-life Activities, N.C.C.B., July 25, 1993.

within marriage are husband and wife given the conditions and grace necessary to begin a family.

Sexuality, by means of which man and woman give themselves to one another through the acts which are proper and exclusive to spouses, is not something simply biological, but concerns the innermost being of the human person as such.It is achieved in a truly human way only if it is an integral part of the love by which a man and a woman commit themselves totally to each other until death.[31] The total physical self-giving would be a lie if it were not the sign and fruit of a total personal self-giving, in which the whole person, including the temporal dimension, is present: if the person were to withhold something or reserve the possibility of deciding otherwise in the future, by this very fact, he or she would not be giving totally.

Sex outside the bonds of marriage involves a selfishness contrary to the plan of God. Sex is seen, not as the giving of oneself exclusively and forever to another, but rather as a satisfaction of a momentary urge or need, no more significant nor important than the urge or need. This is obviously wrong. However, the sexual act between husband and wife, when done in accordance with the plan of God, is both sacred and holy. Used correctly, sex becomes a joyful affirmation of true love between husband and wife.

14. Why does the pleasure of sex before marriage lead to a selfish frustration that destroys real love? When are signs of affection a manifestation of love?

When there is impurity, love is stifled, blinded and questioned: *Do you really love me? Or are you only using me? Do you see the real me or only the pleasure you get from me?* Such questions reveal a love that has already started on the wrong foot. The answer is obvious. Impurity is self-centered and a mere pursuit of pleasure without commitment

31. C.C.C. 2361 and F.C. 11.

or responsibility. Love that was present in the beginning may shrivel up in bitterness and guilt. The link of love and commitment, which should have been building up, is now broken. Through concupiscence a person tends to treat as his own possession another human being, one who does not belong to him but to God.[32]

While dating, a Christian behaves with restraint and dignity, setting a high price for himself or herself—the price that Christ paid for every person with His own redeeming blood.

Do we want a proof of true and serious love? The best proof is heroic purity during dating, while getting to know and evaluating the potential spouse. Signs of affection between unmarried persons are right and good when they are in keeping with the demands of modesty and are true signs of pure love. They must not be actions which arouse passions.

A man and a woman who love one another and who say no to their passions, reserving them for marriage, are saying to each other: *See how truly I love you. I want to honor and dignify you. I want to prove to you that I belong to you.* A valiant commitment to each other is a commitment which God helps and blesses with His own love. If they can take it seriously, they would think: *We will respect and honor each other. She will be my wife, the mother of my children; he will be my husband, the father of my children.*

Personal spiritual guidance and the sacrament of confession can help those who may have doubts about their commitment. God knows human weakness and the pressures of modern culture. Furthermore, it is a sign of maturity and concern for one's future spouse to admit weaknesses and seek forgiveness and advice in overcoming them.

---

32. Cf. L.F. 20.

15. **What are the Christian values and virtues to be fostered during relationships? How can spiritual life be developed? What supernatural means are to be applied?**

Aside from the theological virtues—faith, hope and charity—and the infused moral virtues, there are human virtues.

They develop the personality of each individual. Together with purity, these help form the bedrock upon which the supernatural virtues are built. Marriage will perfect the life of the spouses if they know how to develop Christian virtues from the very beginning of any relationship. Each of these virtues is potentially within each person called to marriage.

Some human virtues are:

- *Generosity.* Forget yourself. Seek the well-being, happiness and spiritual life of the other. Avoid being selfish and doing things your own way.

- *Modesty and decorum.* Guard your senses. Behave correctly in order to avoid temptations or becoming an occasion of sin to others. Do not allow yourself to be wrongly influenced by the environment.

- *Sincerity.* Be truthful with yourself and with each other. Do not try to justify what is wrong. Call a spade a spade.

- *Loyalty to commitments.* Be faithful to each other. Be a model of a Christian relationship. Avoid anything you would be ashamed of before God, your parents, or your family.

- *Making good use of your time.* Idleness is the first source of temptation and can be avoided by planning and using the time you spend together wisely.

The main development of the future spouses' spiritual life is based on their awareness that God is presiding over their hearts. Spiritual growth and progress, to be effective, can be achieved through the following supernatural means:

- *Receiving the sacraments*: Confession and Communion.

- *Prayer*: asking for the necessary graces to behave as a child of God.

- *Self-denial*—especially of the senses and imagination.

- *Devotion to the Blessed Virgin Mary: May I give you some advice for you to put into practice daily? When your heart makes you feel those low cravings, say slowly to the Immaculate Virgin: 'Look on me with compassion. Do not abandon me, my Mother.' And recommend this prayer to others.*[33]

---

33. Josemaría Escrivá. *Furrow*. (Princeton, NJ: Scepter Publishers, Inc., 1975), 849.

C. THE TEACHINGS OF THE CHURCH

> *The husband should fulfill his duty toward his wife, and likewise the wife toward her husband. A wife does not have authority over her own body, but rather her husband, and similarly a husband does not have authority over his own body, but rather his wife.*[34]

16. What is the Catholic concept of Matrimony? Is it always a sacrament?

Matrimony is defined as the *marriage covenant by which a man and woman establish between themselves a partnership of the whole of life is by its nature ordered towards the good of the spouses and the procreation and education of offspring.*[35] For a baptized couple, this covenant has been raised by Christ to the dignity of a sacrament.[36]

17. What does it mean when we say *marriage covenant*?

Marriage covenant is called *covenant* to clearly state the divine nature of that agreement. *Covenant* in the Old Testament refers to the promises and agreements that God made primarily with Abraham and Moses. Since marriage is also an agreement that the spouses make with God to establish a lifetime partnership, there is not a better word to define it.

The model for the holy *covenant* of marriage is the union between Christ and his Church: a mutual love where husband and wife are ready to make sacrifices for each other as Jesus Christ sacrificed himself for the Church and as the Church sacrifices herself to bring souls to Him.[37]

---

34. *1 Corinthians 7:3-4.*
35. Cf. C.I.C. 1055.1 and C.C.C. 1601.
36. Cf. C.C.C. 1601.
37. Cf. C.C.C. 1617 and L.F. 7.

18. Is the Christian *marriage covenant* different from the civil marriage contract?

The *matrimonial covenant* is different from any civil marriage contract. This *covenant* cannot be altered or rescinded at will by the two contracting parties. There is always a third party involved, the author of the contract, God himself.[38]

Contracts established by common agreement of two parties may be altered or rescinded by common agreement. But in marriage, there are three parties involved, and the third party is the one who decides absolutely.[39] Christ said, *What God has joined together, let no one separate* and; *whoever puts away his wife, and marries another, commits adultery; and he who marries a woman who has been put away, commits adultery.*[40] The indissoluble character of marriage is the basis of the common good of the family.[41]

19. Why does the Catholic Church prescribe a set of laws governing marriage?

The Catholic Church has the right to establish laws regarding the validity of marriages since marriage for the baptized is both a covenant and a sacrament. And it is only the Catholic Church that has jurisdiction over those marriages, with due regard for the competence of civil authority concerning the merely civil effects. No one else has the power or authority to change ecclesiastical laws.

20. What are the essential properties of the sacrament of Matrimony?

The essential properties of marriage are *unity* and *indissolubility*.

---

38. Cf. Vatican II and G.S. 48.

39. Cf. C.I.C. 1056 & 1141and C.C.C. 2364. The decision for a marriage to be dissolved could only be done by the Church.

40. *Matthew 19:6, 9.*

41. Cf. L.F. 7.

Unity of marriage signifies that the *covenant* established is between one man and one woman: the husband cannot marry another woman during the lifetime of his wife, nor can the wife marry another man during the lifetime of her husband.

Polygamy—having more than one husband/wife at the same time—is contrary to the equal personal dignity of men and women who in Matrimony give themselves with a love that is total, and therefore, unique and exclusive.[42]

Indissolubility means that the bond of sacramental marriage cannot be broken except by death of either husband or wife.

By virtue of the covenant of married life, the man and woman "are no longer two but one flesh" and they *are called to grow continually in their communion through day-to-day fidelity to their marriage promise of total mutual self-giving.*[43] This union is not simply a physical joining, but a spiritual union of the two souls. While the spouses may be physically apart, the sacrament, once validly contracted, creates a spiritual union that cannot be broken, except by the death of one of the spouses.[44] Moses' permission for men to repudiate their wives in certain circumstances was only a concession to the hardness of their hearts.[45]

The deepest motive for marital fidelity lies in the fidelity of God to his covenant, in that of Christ to his Church. Through the sacrament of Matrimony the spouses are called to represent this fidelity and witness to it. Through the sacrament, the indissolubility of marriage receives a new and deeper meaning.[46]

---

42. Cf. C.C.C. 1645 and F.C. 19.

43. C.C.C. 1644 and F.C. 19.

44. Cf. C.C.C. 1640, 2364, 2382.

45. Cf. C.C.C. 1614.

46. C.C.C. 1647.

21. What are the primary purposes of the *marriage covenant*?

By its own natural character, the matrimonial covenant is ordered toward the good of the spouses and toward the procreation and education of children.[47] *The spouses' union achieves the twofold end of marriage: the good of the spouses and the transmission of life.* These two meanings or values of marriages the unitive and the procreative, cannot be artificially separated without damaging the couple's spiritual life *and compromising the goods of marriage and the future of the family.* The married love of man and woman requires both fidelity and openness to life.[48] The sooner we recognize this fact, and share it with others, the sooner more couples will be able to embrace God's total plan, and be more open to the procreating purpose of marriage.[49]

22. How is true love expressed in marital relations? When is the marital act a sign of authentic love?

True conjugal love is not only exclusive and total, but it is also a fruitful love, both spiritually and physically. Spiritually, it is fruitful because marriage helps the married couple grow in holiness. Physically it is fruitful because the marital act, when done as God wants, gives glory to God and is needed to achieve the *perfect union* between spouses. Some may hold mistaken notions about the Church's teaching on the sacredness of the marital act. Far from being tainted or somehow dirty, as some erroneously think, the Church upholds its dignity.[50]

The acts in marriage, by which the intimate and chaste union of the spouses take place, are noble and honorable;

---

47. Cf. C.I.C. 1055.1.

48. Cf. C.C.C. 2263 and L.F. 12.

49. Cf. Carman Fallace. *Evaluating Marriage and Family Information.* (Lake Grove, NY: Little Flower Publications,1993), p. 7.

50. Cf. C.C.C. 2262 and G.S. 49 and C. & J. Fallace, *Sexual Affection in Marriage.* (Lake Grove, NY: Little Flower Publications,1993).

the truly human performance of these acts fosters the self-giving they signify and enriches the spouses in joy and gratitude.

The Creator himself established that in the generative function, spouses should experience pleasure and enjoyment of the body and spirit. Therefore, the spouses do nothing evil in seeking this pleasure and enjoyment. They accept what the Creator has intended for them. Nevertheless, spouses should know how to keep themselves within the just limits of moderation.[51]

As Blessed Josemaría Escrivá, founder of the Prelature of Opus Dei, wrote: *When love is authentic, it demands faithfulness and rectitude in all marital relations. St. Thomas Aquinas comments that God has joined to the exercise of the different functions of human life a pleasure or satisfaction, which is something good. But if man, inverting the proper order of things, seeks satisfaction as an aim in itself, in contempt of the good to which it is joined and which is its aim, he perverts its true nature and converts it into a sin, or an occasion of sin.*[52]

Even Sigmund Freud says, *It is a characteristic common to all the sexual perversions that in them reproduction as an aim is put aside.*[53] This is actually the criterion by which we judge whether sexual activity is perverse—if it departs from reproduction in its aims and pursues gratification independently.

To keep a genuine love between husband and wife, each marital act must remain open to the transmission of life. Procreation can never be excluded from the marital act because God has willed an inseparable connection between the unifying and the procreative meaning of conjugal love.[54]

51. G.S. 49 and Pius XII, *Discourse*, October 29, 1951 and John Paul II *Address on November 26, 1993.*

52. Josemaría Escrivá. *Christ is Passing By.* (Princeton, NJ: Scepter Publishers, Inc., 1975), 25.

53. John Haas. *Contraception, A Personal Odyssey # 180.* (Princeton, NJ: Scepter Publishers, Inc., 1982).

54. Cf. C.C.C. 2366 and H.V. 11-12.

Responsible parenthood implies openness to life in conjugal relations. An openness to life in conjugal relations protects the very authenticity of the love relationship, saving it from the risk of descending to the level of mere utilitarian enjoyment.[55]

The command of God to our first parents in Genesis to be fruitful and multiply does not require every marital act to have as its goal the conception of life; however, in each marital act there can be no action opposed to the transmission of life.

Every action which, whether in anticipation of the conjugal act, or in its accomplishment, or in the development of its natural consequences, proposes, whether as an end or as a means to render procreation impossible is intrinsically evil.[56]

Contraception, i.e. action against conception, has as its goal the prevention of the transmission of life. This action is a misuse of the reproductive faculties, and it violates one of the purposes of marriage. It is a direct refusal or saying "no" to God's plan for your life and vocation to bring forth new life. It may lead to a loss of faith.

Life itself is sacred, and because of this very fact, sexual intercourse, unlike other physical actions, is itself also sacred. By it, couples share God's creative power and fatherhood.[57]

Considering God as the ultimate cause of all things, it should be kept in mind that *at the origin of every human person there is a creative act of God. No man comes into existence by chance; he is always the object of God's creative love. From this fundamental truth of faith and reason it follows that the procreative capacity, inscribed in human sexuality, is, in its*

---

55. Cf. John Paul II, *Address of December 14, 1990* and Committee Pro-life Activites, N.C.C.B., July 25, 1993.

56. C.C.C. 2370 and F.C. 32.

57. Cf. C.C.C. 2367.

*deepest truth, a cooperation with God's creative power. And it
also follows that man and woman are neither the arbiters of this
capacity, nor its masters.*[58]

*The biological phenomenon of human reproduction, wherein
the human person finds his or her beginning, also has its end in
the emergence of a new person, unique and unrepeatable, made
in the image and likeness of God.*[59]

The use of contraception deprives the marital act of its
sacred nature, saying "no" to the transmission and to the
value of life. This "no" to life leads to selfishness in which
each partner will increasingly tend to use the other to sat-
isfy his or her sensual needs. This "no" also translates to
an increase of material goods, a better career, or comfort at
any cost.

Furthermore, once the primary purpose of sexual relations is excluded, there is little to distinguish it from other
sexual perversions such as premarital sex, masturbation,
etc., which seek as their primary end sensual satisfaction,
without openness to life. Sadly, couples find themselves
growing farther and farther apart. They may not recognize
that the spiritual barrier they have placed between themselves is the real reason for this distance.

23. Can artificial birth control ever be in conformity with Church teachings (e.g. in extreme cases)?

Artificial birth control can never conform to Church teaching, even in extreme cases. To impede the sources of life
is a violation of the law of God, and a misuse of the gifts
which God has granted to mankind. Doing so proves that
a person is moved by fear or selfishness, not by love. Everything becomes clouded because husband and wife begin
to look at each other as accomplices. Ironically, they may
experience less intimacy in the midst of more frequent sexual

58. John Paul II, *Address to Congress on Responsible Procreation, November 17, 1983.*
59. *Ibid.*

acts. The wounds that are created, if this state is allowed to continue, are almost always impossible to heal. Love is no longer authentic.[60] Its use non-verbally communicates: *I accept the part of you which brings pleasure but not the part which brings forth new life.*

The innate language that expresses the total self-giving of husband and wife is overlaid, through contraception, by an objectively contradictory language, namely that of not giving oneself totally to the other. This leads not only to a positive refusal to be open to life, but also to a betrayal of the inner truth of conjugal love, which is called upon to give itself in personal totality.[61]

The Catholic Church prohibits the use of *artificial birth control*, such as the pill, withdrawal, IUD, condom, etc. They can never be used: they contradict the purpose of marriage because they interfere with God's plan and purpose in creating new life. They are intrinsically evil. It is like saying *non serviam* to God (I will not serve you in this capacity).

Conversely: When there is chastity in the love of married persons, their marital life is authentic; husband and wife are true to themselves, they understand each other and develop the union between themselves.[62]

In the conjugal act, husband and wife are called to confirm in a responsible way the mutual gift of self which they have made to each other in the marriage covenant. The logic of the total gift of self to the other involves a potential openness to procreation: In this way the marriage is called to even greater fulfillment as a family. Certainly the mutual gift of husband and wife does not have the begetting of children as its only end, but is in itself a mutual communion of love and of life. The intimate truth of this gift must always be safeguarded. Intimate is not here synonymous with subjective. Rather, it means essentially in conformity with the

60. Cf. *Ibid.*
61. F.C. 32.
62. Cf. John Paul II, *Address of November 13, 1988.*

objective truth of the man and woman who give themselves. The person can never be considered a means to an end; above all never a means of "pleasure." The person is and must be nothing other than the end of every act. Only then does the action correspond to the true dignity of the person.[63]

While some forms of *artificial birth control* have contraception as their goal, the actual result has been abortion. Others, such as the IUD, the pill, or the *morning-after (abortifacient) pills,* e.g. RU-486, are always abortifacients by destroying the new life—the already fertilized egg. These abortifacient methods of "contraception" are especially immoral, because, as life begins at conception, they cause the abortion of a new human life. Life must be always guarded with greatest care: abortion and infanticide are unspeakable crimes. From the moment of conception man is already destined to eternity in God.[64]

The proper use of conjugal relations during marriage is an important key to a successful marriage. Priests with experience in Marriage Tribunals realize that in many cases, divorce is preceded by unchastity—either by contraception during the marriage, premarital sex, extra-marital sex, or by all three.

24. How can chastity be compatible with human affection, sex and love in married life?

God instituted marriage and established rules for chastity in marriage. The decision of following His law will be the best way to be happy in married life. But, how can chastity be compatible with affection and sex in married life?

Let us answer with some words from Blessed Josemaría Escrivá: *With regard to chastity in married life, I can assure all married couples that they need not be afraid of showing affection for each other. On the contrary, this inclination is at the root of*

63. Cf. L.F. 12
64. Cf. C.C.C. 2270; G.S. 51 and L.F. 9.

their family life. What our Lord expects from them is that they should respect each other and that they should be loyal to each other; that they should act with refinement, naturalness and modesty. I must also tell them that the dignity of their conjugal relations is a result of the love that is expressed in them. And there will be love if those relations are open to fruitfulness, to bringing children into the world.[65]

The Catechism of the Catholic Church emphasizes that sexuality is directed to spousal love of man and woman. *In marriage the couple's bodily intimacy becomes a pledge of spiritual communion.*[66]

25. Whom can we ask about all these questions in order to get the right advice?

We always need to look for the right person in order to get the right advice: *Married couples should remember, when they receive advice and recommendations on this matter, that what they have to do is to discover what God wants of them. With sincerity, right intention, and a minimum of Christian formation, our conscience knows how to discover God's will in this sphere as in others. There are cases in which we seek advice that will favor our own selfishness, and suppress with its apparent authority the voice of our inner convictions. Then we even go from adviser to adviser until we find an agreeable one. This is a pharisaical attitude which is unworthy of a child of God.*[67]

26. Is it still a sign of being blessed to have a large family? Are children a source of joy?

Children are the supreme gift of marriage.[68] Sacred Scripture and the Church's traditional practice have viewed large

---

65. Josemaría Escrivá. *Conversations.* (Princeton, NJ: Scepter Publishers, Inc., 1970), 93.

66. Cf. C.C.C. 2360.

67. Josemaría Escrivá. *Conversations.* (Princeton, NJ: Scepter Publishers, Inc., 1970), 93.

68. C.C.C. 1652 and G.S. 50.

families as a sign of God's blessing and the parents' generosity.[69]

Children are always a source of joy when they are born
out of love: *every new child is a new revelation of God's love and
of the fidelity of the spouses. Each child is also a test of our respect
for the mystery of life, upon which, from the very first moment
of conception, the Creator places the imprint of his image and
likeness. This parenthood brings together the human and divine
and leads the spouses to a free and mutual giving of self.[70] They
see, in their children the crowning of the love for each other. They
want children as a priceless gift.[71]*

27. What is the real meaning of responsible parenthood?

*. . . The responsible exercise of parenthood implies that hus-
band and wife fully recognize their own duties towards God,
towards themselves, towards their family, and towards society,
in a correct hierarchy of values.[72] It involves the recognition of
duties to God, themselves, the family and society; while at the
same time recognizing that they are not free to proceed completely at will, as if they could determine in a wholly autonomous
way the honest path to follow; but they must conform their activity to the creative intention of God expressed in the very nature
of marriage and of its acts, and manifested by the constant teaching of the Church.[73]*

This concept of *responsible parenthood* must be correctly
understood. It must be considered under its various legitimate and interrelated aspects.

In relation to the biological processes, *responsible
parenthood* means knowing and respecting the functions of
these processes; the intellect discovers in the power of giv-

---

69. Cf. C.C.C. 1652.

70. John Paul II, *Address to U. S. Bishops of October 24, 1988.*

71. Cf. L.F. 9.

72. Cardinal Ugo Poletti, *Avenire*, March 18, 1988.

73. *Ibid.*

ing life biological laws that are part of the human person.

In relation to the tendencies of instinct and of the passions, *responsible parenthood* means the necessary mastery that reason and will must exercise over them.

In relation to physical, economic, psychological and social conditions, *responsible parenthood* is exercised either by the thoughtfully made and generous decision to raise a large family, or by the decision, made for grave motives and with respect for the moral law, to avoid a new birth for the time being, or even for an indeterminate period.

Responsible parenthood also and above all implies a more profound relationship to the objective moral order established by God, and of which a right conscience is the faithful interpreter.[74]

28. Does God have a definite plan for every couple? What is their responsibility before God? What about couples that cannot have children?

God has a plan for every couple, which includes the number of children which they should offer Him through their marriage. He does not force *His will* on us but wants the couple to freely and responsibly to say yes to His plan.

Responsibility for love and for life! That expression reminds us of the greatness of the vocation of the spouses, called to be free and conscious collaborators of the God who is love, who creates through love and calls to love. Through this sense of responsibility for love and for life, God the Creator invites the spouses not to be passive operators, but rather cooperators or almost interpreters of his plan.[75]

A child is a gift. The most precious gift of marriage is a human person. Yet some couples cannot bear children.

---

74. Cf. C.C.C. 2376 and H.V. 10.

75. John Paul II, *Address of December 14, 1990.*

Physical sterility is not an evil. *Couples who still suffer from infertility after exhausting legitimate medical procedures should unite themselves with the Lord's cross, the source of all spiritual fecundity. They give expression to their generosity by adopting abandoned children or undertaking demanding service to others.* Their marriage can nevertheless have a full meaning, in both human and Christian terms. *Their marriage can radiate a fruitfulness of love, of hospitality and sacrifice.*[76]

29. Is recourse to natural family planning (NFP) compatible with responsible parenthood?

Responsible parenthood is not incompatible with recourse to natural family planning when serious motives exist. But the husband and wife have to take the above considerations into account and weigh the matter conscientiously before God. Such a goal cannot be achieved unless conjugal chastity is sincerely practiced. *For just reasons, couples may want to space the births of their children. It is their duty to make certain that their desire is not motivated by selfishness but is in conformity with the generosity appropriate to responsible parenthood. They should also govern their behavior by the objective criteria of morality.*[77]

It is the married couple who must in the last analysis make the judgment. They should realize that their behavior must be governed by the dictates of a *well-formed conscience,* which may contradict feelings and impulses. Some say that conscience is sacred; indeed, it has been called *man's sanctuary.* Couples must remember why it is sacred: it is where God speaks to them. This conscience conforms to the will of God through the teaching authority of the Church, which is the authentic interpreter of divine law. For the divine law throws light on the meaning of married love, protects it and leads it to truly human fulfillment.

---

76. Cf. C.C.C. 1654, 2378, 2379 and G.S. 50.

77. C.C.C. 2368; cf. G.S. 51.

In this, and not in anything else, lies the entire mystery and the dignity of moral conscience: in being the place, the sacred place where God speaks to man.[78]

What is usually referred to as *Natural Family Planning* (NFP), *the practice of using infertile times for expression of marital love, is available for those who for serious reasons need to postpone a new birth. This practice expresses in a concrete way the right relationship between spouses in marriage. It calls for a profound respect for each other and a communion of minds and hearts regarding the regulation of births. It acknowledges the different, yet complementary, desires and needs of a man and a woman and insists that co-responsibility for decisions regarding children is essential.*

NFP admittedly requires proper initiation, commitment and the full cooperation of husband and wife. It respects human nature and moves beyond mechanical ways of expressing human love. The relationship between communion and generativity is preserved and a new level of understanding between husband and wife is promoted. Such planning builds an atmosphere in which the parents together are also much more inclined to assume coresponsibility for the rearing of their children.[79]

The most *natural* spacing of children comes from the natural breast feeding of an infant since it suppresses ovulation. Without focusing on the "family planning" couples find that their children are nicely spaced.

The reasons that warrant recourse to periodic continence—for spacing births—should be important. There must be serious grounds that take into consideration the obligation of marriage for procreation and education of children according to God's plan.

These reasonable grounds may include the physical or psychological health of the husband or wife, harmony and

78. John Paul II, *The Splendor of the Truth*, no. 58, 1993.

79. O.C.J. 83.

peace of the family, better conditions for education of children already born or external circumstances.[80]

The lawful methods of *Natural Family Planning* are methods like the *temperature method, ovulation method,* and the *sympto-thermo method.* Each of these methods may be used under the following conditions:

- Every marital act must be *open to the transmission of life*: artificial birth control (*i.e. pill,* IUD device, withdrawal, condom, etc.,) masturbation or voluntary sterilization are never allowed since they are serious transgressions of God's law, going against the nature of conjugal love and setting the grounds for the ultimate destruction of the *marriage covenant.*

- The judgment to use NFP should be made with an upright conscience, i.e. a conscience informed by the teachings of the Church.

- The *serious moral motives* must exist at the time when NFP is practiced.

- And, there should be *no occasion of sin* for either of the spouses, for example, danger of infidelity due to long periods of continence. These periods mean respecting the laws of the generative process—to acknowledge oneself not to be the arbiter of the sources of human life, but rather the minister of the design established by the Creator.[81]

- The *advice and guidance of a prudent priest* will always help the couple to make the correct decision before God.

- Also *prohibited is any act for sexual pleasure* that by its nature is not directed or destined for the procreating and uniting aspects of married love, e.g. oral intercourse, self or mutual masturbation, etc.

---

80. Cf. John Paul II, *Address of November 26, 1993* and Paul VI, H.V. 16.
81. Cf. H.V. 16.

The Church severely condemns any alteration of natural law and, for this reason, condemns artificial birth control. The Church's teaching in this matter has always been the same from the very beginning of Christianity.

Moreover, experience has shown that the destruction of the *marriage covenant* may be subtle. The erosion usually occurs over years of contraceptive usage. Contraceptive sex can even become alienating once its original purpose has been removed.

30. What are the most important effects of the sacrament of Matrimony?

The chief effects of the sacrament of Matrimony are:[82]

- An increase of *sanctifying grace* when it is received in the state of grace. Before Matrimony it is necessary to go to the sacrament of Confession when one has mortal sins.

- An *indissoluble bond* of marriage. *A ratified and consummated marriage cannot be dissolved by any human power or for any reason other than death. The bond that is irrevocable gives rise to a covenant guaranteed by God's fidelity.*[83]

31. Is there any special grace that comes with the sacrament of Matrimony? What are the effects of that grace?

There is a special grace of the sacrament of Matrimony that gives husband and wife the supernatural power to:[84]

- Help each other to attain holiness in their married life and to bring up and educate their children.[85]

---

82. Cf. C.I.C. 1134.

83. C.I.C. 1141 and C.C.C. 1640, 2382.

84. Cf. C.C.C. 1641, 1642.

85. Cf. C.C.C. 2367 and G.S. 51.

- Be faithful as long as they live.
- Fulfill their marital rights and duties.
- Bear with each other's faults, until death.
- Perfect their love for each other. It is a *love that is an eminently human one, since it is directed from one person to another through an affection of the will. It involves the good of the whole person. . . . Such love, merging the human with the divine, leads the spouses to a free and mutual gift of themselves. . . . It is a love that involves the gift of the whole person. Included in this gift is their whole sexuality with its openness to the transmission of life.*[86]

32. What is matrimonial consent? Who is capable of getting married?

Matrimonial consent is an act of the will by which a man and a woman, in an irrevocable covenant, mutually give and accept each other, declaring their willingness to welcome children and to educate them. Marital consent defines and consolidates the good common to marriage and to the family.[87]

Consent must be a free act of the will of each of the contracting parties, without coercion or serious fear arising from external circumstances. To be free means:

- *Not to be acting under constraint.*
- *Not impeded by natural or ecclesiastical law.*[88]

Only those capable of giving valid matrimonial consent can get married: Matrimony is created through the consent of the parties, legitimately manifested between persons who, according to law, are capable of giving consent.[89]

---

86. John Paul II, *Address of October 24, 1988.*

87. Cf. C.I.C. 1057.2; C.C.C. 1627 and L.F. 10, 15.

88. Cf. C.I.C. 1103 and C.C.C. 1625, 1628.

89. Cf. C.I.C. 1057.1 and C.C.C. 1626, 1628.

33. **What are the conditions for a valid marriage? Can they be summarized?**

The conditions for a valid marriage in the Church are:

I. The contracting parties must be capable, according to Church law, of giving matrimonial consent. Before Matrimony is celebrated, it must be evident that no impediment stands in the way of its valid and licit celebration.[90] Impediments could arise from:

A. DIVINE LAW

Impediments based on divine law bind everyone and can never be dispensed.

- *Impotence*: antecedent and perpetual physical impossibility to have intercourse, whether on the part of the man or the woman, which is either absolute or relative. Sterility does not forbid, nor invalidate marriage, unless one of the parties is fraudulently deceived in order to obtain consent.[91]

- *Existing Marriage Bond*: as long as the declaration of nullity or dissolution of a previous marriage is not legitimately and certainly established.[92]

- *Consanguinity*: all relatives originating from each other by procreation, whether legitimate or natural in what is called a direct line, for example, father-daughter; and descendants from a common ancestor in a collateral line, up to and including the second degree (brothers and sisters).[93]

B. ECCLESIASTICAL LAW (CHURCH LAW)

Ecclesiastical law binds only baptized Catholics. The local Ordinary (usually the bishop of the diocese) can

90. Cf. C.I.C. 1066.
91. Cf. C.I.C. 1084, 1097, 1098.
92. Cf. C.I.C. 1085.
93. Cf. C.I.C. 1078, 1091.

dispense from *impediments of ecclesiastical law, as often as he judges that the dispensation will contribute to the good of the faithful with the exception of impediments whose dispensation is reserved to the Apostolic See.*[94] That *dispensation may not be granted without a just and reasonable cause and without taking into consideration the circumstances of the case.*[95]

- **Lack of Valid Age**: To be married the Church requires that men have completed their sixteenth year (one completes one's sixteenth year the day after one reaches sixteen years of age) and that women have completed their fourteenth year of age (one completes her fourteenth year of age the day after she reaches fourteen years of age). These ages are the minimum for validity.[96] There may also be civil laws regulating the minimum age for each state and country, but these do not invalidate marriage in the eyes of the Church.

- **Disparity of Cult**: between one baptized in the Catholic Church or who has been received into it and has not left it by means of a formal act and an unbaptized person.[97]

- **Holy Orders**: Those who have been ordained as a deacon or priest cannot attempt marriage.[98]

- **Public Perpetual Vow of Chastity**: in a Religious institute.[99]

- **Abduction**: abduction or at least unlawful detention of a woman for the purpose of marrying her.[100]

94. C.I.C. 88, 1078. A dispensation from the following impediments is reserved to the Apostolic See: holy orders, public perpetual vow of chastity and crime.

95. C.I.C. 90.

96. Cf. C.I.C. 1083.1.

97. Cf. C.I.C. 1086 and C.C.C. 1635.

98. Cf. C.I.C. 1087.

99. Cf. C.I.C. 1088.

100. Cf. C.I.C. 1089.

- *Crime*: bringing about the death of a person's spouse or one's own spouse for the purpose of entering marriage with that person. It could be also the case of bringing about the death of the spouse of one of them through mutual, physical or moral cooperation.[101]

- *Consanguinity*: descendants from a common ancestor in the collateral line of the third and fourth degree (such as aunt and nephew or first cousins).[102] In some states these marriages are not allowed.

- *Affinity*: blood relatives (not relatives by adoption) of the spouse in a previous valid marriage in any degree of the direct line.[103]

- *Public Propriety*: arising from an invalid marriage, after common life has been established, or from notorious and public concubinage, the impediment affects the man and the blood relatives of the woman, and vice-versa, in the first degree of the direct line.[104]

- *Legal Relationship*: arising from adoption, within direct line or in the second degree of collateral line.[105]

A parish priest could clarify and explain the meaning of these impediments.

C. CIVIL LAW

Impediments arising from civil law bind only non-baptized persons. They are established by civil authority.

II. The consent given by the parties must be deliberate, fully voluntary, free, mutual, and public. Therefore, the following are incapable of contracting marriage:

- Persons who lack sufficient use of reason.

---

101. Cf. C.I.C. 1090.
102. Cf. C.I.C. 1091.
103. Cf. C.I.C. 1092.
104. Cf. C.I.C. 1093.
105. Cf. C.I.C. 1094.

- Persons who suffer from grave lack of discretion of judgment concerning essential matrimonial rights and duties which are to be mutually given and accepted.

- Persons who, due to serious psychic illness, cannot assume the essential obligations of Matrimony.[106]

III. The consent must be *legitimately manifested in canonical form*, with the presence of an authorized priest or deacon and in the presence of two witnesses.[107] Canonical form does not oblige non-Catholics when they marry between themselves, but only Catholics—even if only one of the two parties is Catholic—who have not left the Church by a formal act. The bishop, *priest, or deacon who assists at the celebration of a marriage receives the consent of the spouses in the name of the Church and gives them the blessing of the Church. The presence of the Church's minister and also of the witnesses visibly expresses the fact that marriage is an ecclesial reality.*[108]

34. If each requirement for a valid marriage is present, what else is needed for the worthy reception of the Sacrament?

Once the requirements for a valid marriage are fulfilled, some other conditions are needed for the worthy reception of the sacrament of Matrimony:

- Both parties must be *baptized persons*.

- *Rectitude of intention*. Thoughtfulness and prudence are always necessary for the choice of a future spouse. Being carried away by emotions or momentary passions should be avoided. Premarital pregnancy is not a sufficient motive to marry someone since that could involve an added mistake.

106. Cf. C.I.C. 1095.

107. Cf. C.I.C. 1108.

108. Cf. C.C.C. 1630.

- *Spiritual preparation.* One should be in the state of grace. The sacraments of Penance and Holy Eucharist are strongly recommended as immediate preparation. A general confession would be advisable in the case of someone who has been away from the sacrament of Reconciliation for a long time.[109]

- *Having previously received the sacrament of Confirmation.* Otherwise one should receive this sacrament unless grave difficulties arise.

- *Knowledge of the duties of married life.* Such duties include mutual fidelity of the spouses until death and care for the bodily and spiritual welfare of the children sent by God.

- *Obedience to the marriage laws of the Church.*

---

109. Cf. C.C.C. 1622.

D. ARRANGEMENTS FOR THE WEDDING

*On the third day there was a wedding in Cana in Galilee,
and the mother of Jesus was there. Jesus and his disciples
were also invited to the wedding.*[110]

35. Where should the celebration of marriage take place? Who can solemnize the marriage?

Marriages are celebrated in the parish of either the bride
or the groom. Marriages can also be celebrated elsewhere:

- If it is another Church or oratory, then permission
can come from proper Ordinary or pastor;
- If it is another suitable place, then only the proper
Ordinary can grant this permission.

The parties should inform their pastor. Six months no-
tification before marriage is the norm, but local diocesan
policies, which may suggest a lesser or greater time, are to
be observed. The couple should meet with the priest who
will officiate the marriage at least six months before the
wedding. He will instruct them on the specific details of the
wedding ceremony.

The local ordinary or the pastor, within their territory,
or a priest or deacon delegated by either of them, can preside over the marriage.

*In the Latin Rite the celebration of marriage between two
Catholic faithful normally takes place during Holy Mass because
of the connection of all the sacraments with the paschal mystery
of Christ.*[111] In the Eucharist is celebrated the memorial of
the New Covenant, in which Christ is united forever with
the Church, his beloved bride for whom he gave himself

---

110. *John* 2:1-2.
111. C.C.C. 1621; cf. S.C. 61.

up.[112] *It is therefore fitting that the spouses should seal their consent to give themselves to each other by offering their own lives, in union with the offering of Christ for his Church, made present in the Eucharistic sacrifice, and by receiving the Eucharist, so that communicating in the same body and the same blood of Christ they might form only one body in Christ.*[113]

36. What procedures should be followed for a Church marriage?

For a *Church marriage* to be canonically and civilly valid, it should be performed in accord with the Civil and Canon Law. The partners should carefully prepare and follow the procedures required by both the Church and Civil Laws. The requirements and procedures may differ among states and dioceses.

In those places—including the United States of America—where the Church has established an agreement with the government, the *Church marriage* automatically has the civil effects of a *civil marriage.* Only a marriage *license* from the civil authorities is needed.

37. Is it good to go over the Rite of Marriage before the wedding?

Yes. It helps the couple understand the meaning of the Rite of Marriage in which each spouse administers the sacrament of Matrimony to the other.

38. What courses, documents, interviews, or other requirements are needed?

Specific requirements before the wedding ceremony are:

---

112. Cf. C.C.C. 1621 and L.G. 6.
113. Cf. C.C.C. 1621 and *1 Corinthians* 10:17.

I. DOCUMENTS

- *Baptismal certificates* of both parties (even non-Catholics) issued for marriage purposes and dated no earlier than six months prior to the wedding.[114] If this would cause the non-Catholic party problems, a sworn statement of parents, or those who could testify to the baptism, stating that the person was baptized will be sufficient. If this cannot be had, then a dispensation from disparity of cult *ad cautelam* should be had.

- *Marriage license* from the civil registrar's office. It includes: the application of the two parties, the notice (it could take 10 days) and the license itself. The marriage license can be obtained from different civil offices according to state and county law and that different laws apply in different places.

- *Letters of freedom* of pastors and parents.

- *Permission of parents* if a party is under eighteen years of age.

- *Certificate of attendance* at a Seminar for Marriage Instruction as approved by the diocese. That pre-marriage preparation could also have been given by the minister himself or by a parish based team.

- Sometimes a *written permission* from the pastor of the bride is required.

- *For widows and widowers,* an authentic certificate of the death of their departed spouses with whom they were married and a marriage certificate of the previous wedding.

In some states and counties, it is necessary for the priest or deacon to be registered and even bonded before they can witness a marriage. Also, in some dioceses the *name, official residence* and *license number* of the priest

---

114. Cf. C.I.C. 876, whenever a Baptismal Certificate cannot be obtained, a sworn statment will suffice.

or deacon who is going to assist the marriage when he is not the priest of the parish in which the wedding is to be celebrated.

Begin arrangements six months before the wedding, especially for the premarital instruction and the application for certificates and marriage license.

II. PRE-NUPTIAL INQUIRY

To be conducted by the priest of the parish where the wedding will be celebrated before the publication of the banns. The purpose of the inquiry is:

- To ensure that both parties are capable of being validly married: there are neither impediments, nor causes for a defective or vitiated consent.

- To ensure the freedom of the parties in their decision.

- To ensure that the contracting parties are sufficiently instructed in Christian doctrine, particularly on the nature, ends and essential properties of marriage.

III. BANNS have come to mean the publishing or announcing of the public event of marriage in the parishes of the bride and the groom, and in the parish where the wedding will take place. Canonically, however, they are still meant to provide the opportunity for the revealing of possible obstacles for marriage.

Publication of banns may also be done in other parishes when there is a reasonable suspicion of the existence of any matrimonial impediment that would invalidate the celebration of a particular marriage.[115] *All the faithful are obliged to reveal any impediments they are aware of to the pastor or to the local Ordinary before the celebration of the marriage.*[116]

---

115. Cf. C.I.C. 1067.
116. C.I.C. 1069.

The banns may be announced orally, in print, or even posted at the door of the church on three consecutive Sundays or Holy Days of obligation or other days when there is a great presence of faithful. There will be at least a period of two days between the last publication of the banns and the wedding ceremony.

In some dioceses, banns are no longer required.

IV. MISCELLANEOUS ARRANGEMENTS:

Witnesses (sponsors), wedding booklets, choosing the Readings of the Mass, choir, flowers, etc. These arrangements could take up to one month.

The wedding Mass is a joyous celebration, and also a dignified event taking place within the church. The dress of those participating in it should reflect that dignity. The wedding songs should be in accordance with the approved liturgy, not just ordinary songs. The music should be carefully arranged, keeping in mind the nature of the celebration and the norms of the Church. The selection of appropriate music is usually the responsibility of the bride and groom. The pastor, or the music director, can assist in the choice of music.

The church is a place of worship. The conduct of all involved in the wedding should reflect this. Movements and postures during the ceremony as well as guidelines for receiving Communion (see Part III, F) should be followed. Good manners and respect for the beliefs of the Church apply to all those involved (Catholic and non-Catholic alike) during both the rehearsal and the ceremony itself.

Arrangements for those participating in the wedding, such as altar boys, attendants, organists, cantors, flower girls, and other participants, should also be discussed with the priest. There may be some particular parish regulations that should be respected. The priest can usually provide the servers, if requested.

Most parishes allow photographs during the wedding ceremony and also provide ample time for pictures after the wedding. This should be done in such a way that it does not detract from the liturgical celebration.

As there may be several weddings scheduled on the same day, the parish schedule should be respected.

V. GRATUITIES may not always be required but sometimes are clearly established. It is in good taste however to give a donation to the church, in proportion to the amount spent for the overall wedding. If you wish, it is also appropriate to give a stipend to the officiating priest. The organist and other musicians are usually paid a stipulated fee. It is appropriate to give a small donation to the organist, and the altar boys.

VI. TIMETABLE. In Part III, D there is a suggested schedule timetable for the celebration of marriage.

39. Where can one find the official rite for the wedding ceremony? Is it necessary for a valid ceremony?

The official version of the Marriage Rite approved for each country may differ. Some *wedding booklets* include a Rite for Marriage that is not valid in other countries. Consult a parish priest and get a copy of the approved marriage rite from him.

It is absolutely necessary to follow the Rite of Marriage approved by the local bishop or the Bishop's Conference for a valid wedding ceremony.

The Church normally requires the canonical form of marriage for Catholics, for several reasons.[117]

- Sacramental marriage is a *liturgical act*. It is therefore appropriate that it should be celebrated in the public liturgy of the Church.

---

117. Cf. C.C.C. 1631.

- Marriage introduces the bride and the groom into an ecclesial order and creates rights and duties in the Church between the spouses and toward their children.

- Since marriage is a *public state of life* in the Church, there must be certitude about this marriage; hence the need for witnesses.

- Its public character protects the consent given and helps the spouses remain faithful to it.

E. FAMILY LIFE

Wives, be subordinate to your husbands, as is proper in the Lord. Husbands, love your wives, and avoid any bitterness toward them. Children, obey your parents in everything, for this is pleasing to the Lord. Fathers, do not provoke your children, so they may not become discouraged.[118]

40. Who are the children's primary educators? Is the home the first school of Christian life?

Parents are their children's primary educators. *The fruitfulness of married love extends to the moral, spiritual and supernatural life that parents hand on to their children by education.* The family is a community of persons whose proper way of existing and living together is *communion.*[119] The fundamental task of the family is to serve life, to actualize in history the original blessing of the Creator—that of transmitting by procreation the divine image from person to person.[120]

In giving themselves to each other and to their children, married couples give themselves to God. *In this domestic church, the father, mother, children, and all family members exercise the priesthood of the baptized in a privileged way in receiving the sacraments, in prayer and thanksgiving, in the witness of a holy life, and in self-denial and active charity.*[121] *Thus the home is the first school of Christian life and a school for human enrichment. Here one learns endurance and the joy of work, family love, generous—even repeated—forgiveness and above all divine worship by prayer and the offering of one's life.*[122]

---

118. *Colossians 3:18-21.*
119. C.C.C. 1653; cf. G.E. 3 and L.F. 7.
120. Cf. C.C.C. 1651, 1653 and F.C. 28.
121. G.S. 52.1.
122. Cf. C.C.C. 1657 and L.G. 10.

41. How can children be trained for a future successful marriage?

The approach that young people have toward marriage is a very important factor in the success of family life. They need to understand that marriage is a vocation requiring practical preparation. The best school for marriage is the home. Family life is where young people are educated for their future marriage. As Pope John Paul II writes:

Remote preparation begins in early childhood, in that wise family training which leads children to discover themselves as being endowed with a rich and complex psychology and with a particular personality with its own strength and weakness. . . .[123]

Proximate preparation will present marriage as an interpersonal relationship of a man and a woman that has to be continually developed, and will encourage those concerned to study the nature of conjugal sexuality and responsible parenthood, with the essential medical and biological knowledge connected to it.[124]

42. Are there some guidelines for Christian parents?

These guidelines could help not only to preserve unity, but also to make bright and cheerful homes.

- *Self-giving* is at the very heart of marriage. You serve one another, often sacrificing your own wants for the other's good. In order to achieve the common good of the family one must take up the cross and carry it with love.[125] Marriage is for the mature man, who knows that his life and work are at the disposal of his wife and children, and for the mature woman, who knows that her life and work are the care and the service she gives to her husband and children.

123. Cf. F.C. 66.
124. Cf. C.C.C. 1632.
125. Cf. L.F. 10 and F.W.L. N.C.C.B., Origins vol. 23, no. 25.

- *Have a generous disposition* in the challenge of *responsible parenthood.* The institution of marriage and conjugal love are oriented by their very nature to the procreation and education of the offspring. *Children are the supreme gift of marriage.*[126] Give children time, attention, affection, and above all, respect.

- *Respect your spouse.* The person to whom you are married is a child of God, made in his image and likeness. By your marriage, your spouse shares with you a union that was established by God himself and raised by Christ to the dignity of a sacrament. You share in a union that is a vocation to holiness and a means for eternal salvation. To a great extent, for a husband, his wife is his way to heaven; for a wife, her husband is her way to heaven; for both of them, their children are their way to heaven.

- *Trust each other completely.* Suspicion damages love. It is a duty of justice to trust one's closest neighbor and friend, in this case, your spouse. To judge without evidence and to give in to jealousy is a sin—a sin against justice as well as charity.

- *Do things together.* Husband and wife should find happiness and contentment within their own home and in the company of their children. Their first preference for company should be each other and their children. Sharing keeps parents and children united. To be able to share yourself—good and bad qualities—within a family and to be accepted there is indispensable to forming a close relationship with the Lord.[127]

- *Make the home pleasant.* Husband and wife have a responsibility to make their home bright and cheerful, a place made pleasant by their presence and by their interest in everything related to the family. The

---

126. C.C.C. 1652.

127. Cf. F.W.L. N.C.C.B., *Origins* vol. 23, no. 25.

house should be clean and orderly, while allowing children to work and play with naturalness and spontaneity. Meals should be well-prepared, well-balanced and adequate but not lavish. You also come together when tragedy strikes and in joyful celebration of the sacraments.[128]

- *Forgive and seek reconciliation.* Over and over, you let go of old hurts and grudges to make peace with one another.[129] The rule of saying nothing if you cannot praise applies pertinently and relevantly to one's spouse. Correct your spouse, but privately and prudently. Never nag, bicker and criticize him/her in public and certainly not in the presence of the children.

- *Try not to fight or argue.* Arguments tend to obscure rather than clear the issues. Often the spouse who argues the louder is the one who is wrong. Married people should learn to control their temper, and not fight or argue in front of the children who may be hurt, traumatized or disedified by such behavior. As they begin to date in their later years, children who have witnessed their parents regularly fighting and arguing will tend to accept such behavior from potential spouses, continuing a cycle.

- *Have the right attitude toward sex.* Sexuality is directed to the conjugal love of man and woman.[130] God created sex for the procreation of children and total mutual self donation.[131] The pleasure connected with sex is meant by God to attract husband and wife to cooperate with him in transmitting human life, while fostering unity and intimacy between them. It is of God's gifts to a married couple. For a married couple, sex is the expression of mutual self-giving which

---

128. Cf. *Ibid.*

129. Cf. *Ibid.*

130. Cf. C.C.C. 2360.

131. Cf. Pius XI, *Casti connubii, 24* and C. & J. Fallace, *Sexual Affection in Marriage.* (Lake Grove, NY: Little Flower Publications,1993)

fosters and enriches their love for one another and for God. The marital act, within a valid marriage and carried out according to God's plan, is a source of sanctification and merit.

- *Use family money wisely.* Money is meant to serve the well-being of everyone in the family. It should be used a another means of growing in generosity and temperance.

- *Take care of your personal spiritual formation.* There is progress in marriage when both husband and wife know and practice the Catholic faith. A little time reading the Bible and a book about Christ and the Catholic faith will nourish this spiritual formation. Within the family, parents should be the first to preach the faith to their children by their word and example, and should encourage the vocation proper to each, especially a vocation to a sacred state. By fostering spiritual growth, children will listen to God's call and be open to God's grace.[132]

- *Pray together.* You thank God for blessings, reaching for strength, asking for guidance in crisis and doubt. God answers prayers but sometimes in unexpected ways.[133] Praying together was blessed by Our Lord himself when he promised his presence wherever two or three are gathered together praying in His name.[134] Always say grace at meals. Also, the family Rosary is a beautiful prayer as well as a true bond with the Blessed Virgin Mary, Mother of God and our Mother.

- *Affirm life.* Life is a precious gift from God. You oppose whatever destroys life such as murder, abortion, suicide, euthanasia, etc.[135] The most effective

132. Cf. F.W.L. N.C.C.B., Origins vol. 23, no. 25.
133. *Ibid.*
134. Cf. *Matthew 18:19-20.*
135. Cf. F.W.L. N.C.C.B., Origins vol. 23, no. 25.

weapon against anti-life forces is the welcome that families give to new life.

43. Who is responsible for the quality of home life and the well-being of the children? Should the wife work outside the home?

Both parents must oversee the well-being of their children and the quality of home life; both must face decisions pertaining to their respective duties and responsibilites of parenting in relation to work inside and outside the home. Mothers have a particular and often difficult road to follow.

Recent teachings of the popes and bishops stress that *society must be structured in such a way that wives and mothers are not compelled to work outside the home and that their families can live and prosper in a dignified way even when they themselves devote their full time to their own family.*

In addition, the woman has a right to the honor and joy of motherhood as a gift from God and in due course the children also have a right to the care and concern of those who have begotten them, their mothers in particular.[136]

God made men and women equal in personal dignity and responsibility. That equality justifies a woman's access to public functions in society. In a society where a large percentage of women are working mothers, it is often easy to confuse one's role as career woman, wife and mother. However, the choice of a career may be made in a way that is not inconsistent with a woman's femininity, and her role as a wife and mother. Part-time work and maternity leave may be beneficial for the good of the family. However, she must constantly be on the alert for fatigue, a shift in priorities, and a realization of her pivotal role in the home.

---

136. F.C. 23 and John Paul II, *Address of March 24, 1994.*

It is one thing for women to choose to work in the marketplace to enhance their personal growth, to meet financial responsibilites and to contribute their gifts; it is quite another to be compelled to work because of economic necessity. The marketplace and popular culture tend to pull parents away from each other and their children. The Church reminds them of the intimate, irreplaceable and personal nature of work within the home. This irreplaceable role of women, as wife and mother, must be appreciated and recognized as such.

While speaking about employment in reference to the family, it is appropriate to emphasize how important and burdensome is the work women do within the family unit: that work should be acknowledged and deeply appreciated. The toil of a woman who, having given birth to a child, nourishes and cares for that child and devotes herself to its upbringing, particularly in the early years, is so great as to be comparable to any professional work. This ought to be clearly stated and upheld, no less than any other labor right. Motherhood, because of all the hard work it entails, should be recognized as giving the right to financial benefits at least equal to those of other kinds of work undertaken in order to support the family during such a delicate phase of its life.[137]

Women's work within the family home must be recognized and respected as a value in its own right. As always, what a wife and husband decide in this regard must be evaluated in the light of the good of the entire family.

44. What can be the most meaningful job for a wife and mother?

To serve the family—organizing and running a household—can be the most meaningful and fulfilling task of a married woman. Modern equipment and the able help of

137. Cf. L.F. 17; John Paul II, *Address of March 24, 1994* and O.C.J. 69.

husband and children can possibly simplify this task.
Moreover, the establishment of priorities; the management,
informed by her professional study in child development,
nutrition and social skills as well as her experiences are
vital to a happy family.

As Blessed Josemaría Escrivá said: *Women are called to
bring to the family, to society, and to the Church characteristics
which are their own and which they alone can give: their gentle
warmth and untiring generosity, their love for detail, their quick
wit and intuition, their simple and deep piety, their constancy.
A woman's femininity is genuine only if she is aware of the beauty
of this contribution, for which there is no substitute—and if she
incorporates it into her own life.*[138]

---

138. Josemaría Escrivá. *Conversations.* (Princeton, NJ: Scepter Publishers, Inc.,
    1970), 93.

F. DIVORCE, SEPARATION AND INVALID MARRIAGES

> *To the married, however, I give this instruction, not I, but the Lord: a wife should not separate from her husband—and if she does separate she must either remain single or become reconciled to her husband—and a husband should not divorce his wife.*[139]

45. If marriage is permanent, why are some marriages declared invalid—null and void—after some years? Who can do it? Is there such a thing as annulment in the Church?

Marriage is permanent because God established it so from the very beginning.[140] The indissolubility of marriage is for the good of husband and wife, their children and human society as a whole.

The civil government has no power to dissolve a valid marriage—even if the marriage is between non-Catholics. The government can only dissolve the civil aspects of marriage, such as ownership of property, custody of the children, etc. *Even when civil divorce* is allowed by the country's law, marriage, in God's eyes, still exists.

The Church does not have the power to dissolve a valid, sacramental marriage which has been *consummated*. She may only declare a marriage *null and void* upon investigation and evidence that the marriage did not exist from the very beginning. The reasons could be one of the following:

- Lack of a fully *voluntary and free consent*.
- Some deficiency in the *form of the marriage celebration*.
- The presence of *impediments* that make marriage invalid.

---

139. *1 Corinthians 7:10-11.*
140. *Cf. Mark 10:6-9.*

The *declaration of nullity* (so-called *annulment*) is a very important decision of an ecclesiastical court. A very careful investigation has to be made by the court before that conclusion is reached, insuring that no valid marriage is declared *null and void* by mistake.

Strictly speaking, the word *"annulment"* is incorrect since the Church can never annul a valid marriage that was consummated. To annul means to nullify—to make something *null and void*. The word *"annulment"* may seem to imply that the contract made *null and void* was valid before, but this is not the case.

The Church cannot make a valid marriage *null and void*. Nevertheless, people today use the word *"annulment"* instead of *declaration of nullity* to say that there was never a marriage. In that case, *annulment* of a marriage means that there was never a valid *marriage contract* since the necessary conditions were lacking.

When an annulment petition is filed in a Church Marriage Court, both partners must consider their marriage valid until the contrary is declared. Therefore, before dating or courting, considering a new union, the original union must first be declared null and void by a *Church Marriage Tribunal*.

The Church is the only authority which can declare a marriage invalid from the very beginning. The *Church Marriage Tribunal*, after thoroughly examining the case, may declare the *presumed* marriage *null and void* (invalid). In other words, the marriage never existed, even if one or both partners were acting in good faith. Only if the marriage is declared invalid are the parties free to marry again. In this case, there is no question of granting a divorce, but simply declaring the *nullity* or non-existence of a previously *presumed marriage*.[141]

---

141. Cf. C.I.C. 1071, 1095-1107 and C.C.C. 1629.

A *putative marriage*, is an invalid marriage which has been celebrated in good faith by at least one of the parties. The children born of such a union are legitimate.[142]

46. What is the meaning of the unbreakable bond of marriage?

There are cases in which a *civil divorce* is filed and granted. All Christians should keep in mind that a decree of *civil divorce* does not change the status of husband and wife as married persons before God. It does not give either the right to date or to keep company with a third party. They remain married as long as they both shall live. A *ratified and consummated marriage cannot be dissolved by any human power or by any cause other than death.*[143] *Ratified marriage* is understood to be a union approved by the Church as a *valid sacramental covenant.*

If one of the spouses is the innocent victim of a civil divorce, he or she does not violate the moral law.[144] There is in fact a difference between those who have sincerely tried to save their first marriage and have been unjustly abandoned, and those who through their own grave fault have destroyed a canonically valid marriage.[145]

47. What is the difference between separation and divorce? Is there any possibility of dissolving a valid marriage?

Civil divorce is an attempt to break the marriage bond. It is absolutely forbidden by God's law, which binds all men and women, and not just Christians.

Some people point out that the Scripture gives an exception for allowing *divorce,* when Our Lord said, *Whoever*

---

142. Cf. C.I.C. 1137.

143. Cf. C.I.C. 1141 and C.C.C. 1640, 2382.

144. Cf. C.C.C. 2286.

145. Cf. C.C.C. 2386 and F.C. 84.

divorces his wife, except for uncleanness, and marries another, commits adultery.[146] This should be interpreted consistently with Christ's other commands concerning marriage.[147]

In opposition to the Mosaic law, which allowed *divorce* and *remarriage*, Christ insisted in the Gospels on the *indissolubility* of marriage. To be consistent with Christ's entire teachings on marriage, this verse has to be understood in a way which allows for only a legal separation for a spousal violation of marriage, not the freedom to *divorce* and remarry at will. Where there is a legal separation, the parties are still married; and although they live apart, their marriage bond remains unbroken.

Separation of spouses in a valid marriage, without good reason, is a grave offense to the will of God. This is so for the following reasons:

- It deprives the children of proper education, of a home atmosphere and of the love which they have the right to receive.

- It exposes the separated persons to temptation against chastity that could lead to adultery and other sins.

For a very serious reason, however, a validly married person may be allowed to separate from his or her spouse.[148] There are some situations in which living together in marriage becomes impossible to practice for various reasons. *In such cases, the Church permits the physical separation of the couple and their living apart. The spouses do not cease to be husband and wife before God and so are not free to contract a new union.*[149]

---

146. *Matthew 19:9.*

147. Cf. *Mark 10:11-12.*

148. Cf. C.C.C. 2383.

149. Cf. C.I.C. 1151-1155; C.C.C. 1649 and F.C. 83.

Except in extraordinary cases—such as immediate threat of physical harm—no one should make a decision about separation without first consulting a learned priest.

However the Church may only *dissolve* a marriage:

- When it is a natural—not sacramental—bond of a legitimate and consummated marriage of non-baptized parties. This is known as the Pauline privilege.[150] The previous marriage is not dissolved by the Church but by the second marriage itself. The Church just judges that the necessary conditions for the second marriage are present.

- When it is a natural—not sacramental—bond of a legitimate and consummated marriage between a baptized party and a non-baptized party. This is known as the Petrine privilege.

- When it is a non-consummated marriage between baptized persons or between a baptized party and a non-baptized party. Such a marriage can only be dissolved for a just cause, at the request of both parties or one of the parties, even if the other party is unwilling. A decision of this nature can only be made at the discretion of the Roman Pontiff.[151]

48. Can Catholic couples who were married in the Church get a divorce? Why is it a very sinful action?

Divorce, as a breaking of the *marriage contract*, is always banned for any Christian. It is a serious offense against natural law.[152]

---

150. Cf. C.I.C. 1143 and 1 *Corinthians 7:12-15*.

151. Cf. C.I.C. 1142. In some exceptional cases, the Church, not the State may also dissolve a *ratified* though *not consummated* marriage among Christians through Papal decision.

152. Cf. C.C.C. 2384 and 2385.

This sinful action gives way to:

• Introducing disorder into family and society.
• Traumatizing children by the separation of the parents.
• Making marriage a temporary union which goes against the essence of the *marriage contract*.
• Increasing the rate of marriage breakdowns by spreading a contagious divorce mentality to the community.

The apparent difficulty—even impossibility—of binding oneself for life to another human being *makes it all the more important to proclaim the good news that God loves us with a definitive and irrevocable love . . . . Spouses who with God's grace give this witness, often in very difficult conditions, deserve the gratitude and support of the Church community.*[153]

Civil divorce, which is *not* a breaking of the marriage contract, is sometimes allowed to Catholics just for civil effects to protect the innocent. In those cases, they have to refrain from becoming involved in a new union and devote themselves solely to carrying out their family duties and the responsibilities of Christian life. Their example of fidelity and Christian consistency takes on particular value as a witness before the world and the Church.[154]

49. What is the status before God of those who have remarried after getting divorced?

Since the marriage bond is unbreakable, people who are divorced should continue with the obligation of carrying out the family duties and responsibilities. They cannot become involved in a new union since they are still married before God. For that reason those who undergo divorce and try to contract a new marriage end up living in adultery.

---

153. Cf. C.C.C. 1648 and F.C. 28.
154. Cf. C.C.C. 2386 and F.C. 83.

Today in many countries many Catholics have had recourse to civil divorces and have contracted new civil unions. The Church does not recognize a new union as valid, if previous marriage still exists. This is in fidelity to the words of Jesus Christ: *Whoever divorces his wife and marries another, commits adultery against her; and if she divorces his wife and marries another, commits adultery.*[155] *Contracting a new union, even if it is recognized by civil law, adds to the gravity of the rupture: the remarried spouse is then in a situation of public and permanent adultery.*[156]

50. Can one marry a divorced person? Will it be an invalid marriage?

A Christian can never marry a divorced person, whose marriage was *valid and consumated* and whose spouse is still alive. Christ said: *Whoever puts away his wife, and marries another, commits adultery; and he who marries a woman who has been put away, commits adultery.*[157]

In spite of the clear doctrine written in the Gospels, daily experience unfortunately shows that people who have obtained a divorce often intend to enter a new union not in the Church.[158] This new union is clearly an invalid union since the first marriage still exists. A divorced person is still a married person.

51. What about getting married to someone who has been separated or civilly divorced for a long time without hope for reconciliation?

Even in the case where someone has been separated or civilly divorced from the partner for a long time without any possibility of reconciliation, the marriage bond contin-

155. *Mark 10:11-12.*
156. Cf. C.C.C. 1650 and 2384.
157. *Matthew 9:9.*
158. Cf. C.C.C. 2384 and F.C. 84.

ues to exist. It can also happen that one of the partners enters into a new invalid union. Even in this case, the other partner cannot do the same, since the first marriage bond is unbreakable.

G. INTERRELIGIOUS MARRIAGES

> *If any brother has a wife who is an unbeliever, and she is willing to go on living with him, he should not divorce her; and if any woman has a husband who is an unbeliever, and he is willing to go on living with her, she should not divorce her husband. For the unbelieving husband is made holy through his wife, and the unbelieving wife is made holy through the brother.*[159]

52. Can a Catholic marry a non-Catholic? How? What are the special requirements for interreligious marriages? Are they required to marry in the Catholic Church?

Marriages between a Catholic and a baptized Christian who is not in full communion with the Catholic Church are called *mixed marriages*. For *mixed marriages* permission from the local Ordinary, not dispensation, is required for validity. Marriages between Catholics and unbaptized persons (*disparity of cult*) are invalid unless a dispensation from the local Ordinary is granted.[160]

All of this presupposes that these marriages are celebrated with all other necessary conditions.

The local bishop may grant permission or dispensation for such marriages on the following conditions:[161]

- The Catholic party declares that he or she is prepared to remove dangers of falling away from the faith and makes a sincere promise to do all in his or her power to have all the children baptized and brought up in the Catholic Church.[162]

---

159. *1 Corinthians 7:12-14.*

160. Cf. C.I.C. 1124; C.C.C. 1633, 1637 and *Statement on the Implementation of the Apostolic Letter on Mixed Marriages no. 14-15.* N.C.C.B., November 16, 1970.

161. Cf. C.C.C. 1635.

162. Cf. C.C.C. 1635, 1637; C.I.C. 1125.

- The other party is to be informed at an appropriate time of these promises which the Catholic person has to make. It is important that the other person be truly aware of the commitments and obligations of the Catholic spouse.

- Both persons are to be instructed on the essential ends and properties of marriage, which are not to be excluded by either party.

- They should *marry in the Catholic Church*. The canonical form (Church ceremony with an authorized Catholic priest or deacon and at least two other witnesses) is to be followed. When there are serious difficulties the local bishop may give a dispensation and allow a form which is public to be followed. However, it is never allowed to have the Catholic priest or deacon and a non-Catholic minister, rabbi or public official, each performing his own rite, asking for the consent of the parties. Likewise, it is forbidden to have another religious marriage ceremony before or after the Catholic ceremony for giving or receiving the matrimonial consent.[163] Marriage consent is given only once.

53. Are interreligious marriages advisable?

The perfect union of persons and full communion of life which constitutes the married state are more easily assured when both partners belong to the same faith community. In addition, practical experience and the observations obtained in various dialogues between representatives of churches and ecclesial communities indicate that mixed marriages frequently present difficulties for the couples themselves and for the children born to them in maintaining their Christian faith and commitment, and for the harmony

---

163. Cf. C.I.C. 1117, 1127, 1129.

of family life. For all these reasons, marriage between persons of the same ecclesial community remains the objective to be recommended and encouraged.[164]

A number of these particular difficulties faced by Catholics and other Christians in mixed marriages result from the division among Christians:[165]

- The essential properties of marriage—*unity and indissolubility*—are at stake because *divorce* is admitted by most non-Catholics.

- It becomes difficult to give the children a Catholic education since the parents do not share the same ideals and the same rules of morality.

- It could present a *danger to the faith* of the Catholic party.

- Since one of the spouses is not in full communion with the Catholic Church, it would be difficult for him or her to comprehend the value of the sacrament. Furthermore, the Rite of Marriage cannot include the reception of Holy Communion by both parties in the Nuptial Mass.

In view, however, of the growing number of mixed marriages in many parts of the world, the church includes within its urgent pastoral solicitude couples preparing to enter, or already having entered, such marriages.[166] Mixed marriages can be contracted, but the Catholic party has to meditate in the presence of God about the pertinent dangers and ask for the advice of a learned priest.

---

164. Cf. C.C.C. 1634-1636 and *Statement on the Implementation of the Apostolic Letter on Mixed Marriages*, November 16, 1970.

165. Cf. C.I.C. 1126; C.C.C. 1634-1636 and *Statement on the Implementation of the Apostolic Letter on Mixed Marriages*, November 16, 1970.

166. Cf. *Ibid.* and C.C.C. 1633.

H. CIVIL MARRIAGES AND CHURCH MARRIAGES

But it becomes all such as are married, whether men or women, to come together with the consent of the bishop, so that their marriage may be according to godliness . . .[167]

54. Is civil marriage a good starting point for a future marriage?

Civil marriage between a baptized Catholic and another person, whether Catholic or not, is not a valid *marriage contract* before God. It will never be a good starting point for a future marriage in the Church since it is a grave sin.

55. What is the situation of those Catholic couples who are only civilly married? Is it true that they are not married before God? Are they living in sin? Can they go to Communion?

The decision of Catholics who choose to have merely a *civil marriage*, rejecting or deferring the *Church marriage*, is not acceptable. There is no consistency between their choice of life and the Catholic faith which they profess.

When a Catholic contracts a *civil marriage* with another person, Catholic or non-Catholic, the Church does not recognize such a marriage as valid. The couple is not married in the eyes of God. If they live together as husband and wife, they will be in the state of habitual sin and the Church regrettably will not be able to admit them to the sacraments.[168]

---

167. *Epistle of Ignatius to Polycarp* 2:10.
168. Cf. F.C. 82. Here we are not considering the exceptional cases in which the Church granted a dispensation from canonical form and authorizes some public form of celebration.

56. What should a Catholic do who has only been civilly married?

Any Catholic who has only been civilly married should be encouraged to repent and embrace Christ's teaching on marriage. The Church does not ignore persons in such situations. It invites them to a deeper understanding of the meaning and beauty of Catholic marriage and offers them forgiveness. They should seek the sacrament of penance and the advice of a priest as to how the situation can be corrected before God.

57. Is living together a suitable preparation for marriage? Why does the Church forbid trial marriage?

Living together, even in a "trial marriage", with the idea or possibility of getting married later is poor preparation for marriage from a psychological standpoint. Since there is not total commitment, many times the fear of being left by the partner becomes the obstacle for an everlasting union. The Church for her part, cannot admit such union, for further and original reasons which derive from faith.

In the first place, the gift of the body in the sexual relationship is a real symbol of the giving of the whole person: such a giving, moreover, in the present state of things cannot take place, with full truth, without the concourse of the love of charity, given by Christ.

In the second place, marriage between two baptized persons is a real symbol of the union of Christ and the Church, which is not a temporary or trial union but one which is eternally faithful. Between two baptized persons there can exist only an indissoluble marriage.[169]

58. How can a man and a woman get engaged or committed to one another without getting married in the Church? What is *betrothal*?

169. Cf. C.C.C. 2391 and F.C. 82.

The Church has provided a way, although now used infrequently, of making a promise of marriage before the wedding ceremony. It is called *betrothal*, which is a bilateral promise, between a man and a woman, to enter into a sacramental covenant of marriage. This is not a marriage, but it solidifies the commitment of both to marry.

An appropriate ceremony of betrothal may be observed, taking into account the local customs and laws of the land. The obligation to fulfill the promise ceases upon the option of both parties, or even one of them, according to the provisions of the Code of Canon Law.[170]

Betrothal, within the time specified by the same parties, is regulated by a particular law established by the conference of bishops.

59. What are some reasons serious enough to justify calling off a wedding after everything has been prepared?

Marriage is for life. The decision to get married must be prayerfully considered. Any serious and just reason, in the eyes of God, is enough for postponing it or deciding not to get married. It is better to break the relationship in time, than get married and have a life of mutual unhappiness.

60. What are some right and wrong reasons for getting married?

People want to get married for different reasons. First, let us summarize some right reasons, looking at marriage as a sacrament:

- To establish a *Christian family*. Marriage is a Christian vocation to holiness, a real supernatural calling from God. The aim of any marriage is to sanctify family life: to make the members happy children of God on earth, and to bring them eventually to heaven.

---

170. Cf. C.I.C. 1062.2.

- To establish a real *community of life and love;* a Christian family in which all try to love one another as Christ has loved us. That authentic love means sincerity, purity of intention, self-denial and above all faithfulness.

- To offer God as many children as He has willed. Love in sexual relations is shown when these relations are always open to a new life: *A large family—if such is the will of God—is a guarantee of happiness.*[171]

- To fulfill, with joy, the duties as father and husband or the duties as mother and wife. The man has to be ready to spend time with his wife and children, to be a friend of each of them. They must be important to him—more important than business, work or rest.[172] The wife also has to be ready to forgo business, work and rest or to renounce a professional career when necessary for the good of the family and the education of the children.

There are also wrong reasons which cause people to seek marriage. Some of them are as follows:

- To run away from home.

- Only physical attraction.

- Because your family wants you to marry a specific person and you do not know how to say "no."

- Because the woman is afraid of being an unwed mother or the man feels that he is obliged to marry a woman because she is pregnant.

61. What are some desirable qualities to look for in a lifetime partner?

If you want to have a *happy marriage,* there are several key ideas to keep in mind:

---

171. Josemaría Escrivá. *Christ is Passing By.* (Princeton, NJ: Scepter Publishers, Inc., 1975), 25.

172. Cf. *Ibid.* 27 and C.C.C. 2207.

- *Seek someone who strives to a be a good Catholic, responsible, industrious, sincere and loyal.* Choose someone who is chaste and who values the virtue of purity very much. This will assure that he/she values you as a person, not as a sexual partner. Compatibility of characters and mutual knowledge, especially of weaknesses and defects, are important factors.

- *Consider marriage as a vocation to holiness* in the context of which some human virtues have to be developed:

  - *Be eager to receive ongoing formation* about the Catholic faith and teachings on marriage and family life.

  - *Make family life pleasant;* always be gentle and kind.

  - *Have a life full of optimism and joy,* for you need the right outlook.

  - *Have a sense of order,* since order leads to God.

  - *Exercise self-denial and forgetfulness of yourself* so you can give yourself—the real secret of love.

  - *Be generous,* especially in accepting as many children as God sends.

  - *Try always to be patient* in time of trial.

  - *Be understanding,* have a heart that loves everyone at home.

  - *Be willing to forgive,* again and again, and determine if he/she is so willing.

  - *Practice loyalty,* which is a mutual and exclusive love between husband and wife.

PART III

APPENDICES

A. Regulations Regarding Interreligious Marriages

1. Dispensation for the valid celebration of an interreligious marriage in which one party is Catholic and the other unbaptized (*disparity of cult*), may be obtained from the local Ordinary for a just and reasonable cause.

2. Permission for the licit celebration of marriage between a Catholic and a baptized Christian who is not in full communion with the Catholic Church (*mixed marriage*) may be obtained, at least in some dioceses, from the pastor concerned or possibly from a parish priest as well in virtue of delegated faculties.[173] In order to judge the existence or otherwise of a just and reasonable cause with regard to granting permission for *mixed marriages*, the local Ordinary will take account, among other things, of an explicit refusal—of the essential ends and properties of marriage—on the part of the non-Catholic party.[174]

3. Before the celebration of an interreligious marriage, it is good for the contracting parties to be instructed on the essential ends and properties of marriage which are not to be excluded by either party. Furthermore, the Catholic party will be asked to affirm, in the form established by the particular law of the Eastern Catholic churches or by the episcopal conference, that he or she is prepared to avoid the dangers of abandoning the faith and to promise sincerely to do all in his/her power to see that the children of the marriage be baptized and educated in the Catholic Church. The other partner is to be informed of these promises and responsibilities.

---

173. Cf. C.I.C. 1086.2, 1124, 1125, 1126 and Paul VI, *Apostolic Letter, Determining Norms for Mixed Marriages*, nn. 3-5.66.

174. Cf. C.I.C. 1086.2; Sacred Congregation for the Doctrine of the Faith, *Letter, April 30, 1986*, N. 24787 and D.E. 150 Origins vol. 23 no. 9.

No precise manner or occasion of informing the non-Catholic is prescribed.[175]

4. The declaration and promise of the Catholic necessary to gain dispensation for an interreligious marriage shall be made, in the following words or their substantial equivalent:

    I reaffirm my faith in Jesus Christ and, with God's help, intend to continue living that faith in the Catholic Church.

    I promise to do all in my power to share the faith I have received with our children by having them baptized and reared as Catholics.

    This declaration and promise are to be made in the presence of a priest or deacon either orally or in writing, as the Catholic prefers.[176]

5. In the case of *mixed marriages* the positive aspects of what the couple share together as Christians in the life of grace, in faith, hope and love, along with the other interior gifts of the Holy Spirit should be stressed.[177]

6. The canonical form of the celebration of marriage, required for validity, is to be observed in interreligious marriages. Where there are serious difficulties in observing the canonical form in a *mixed marriage,* the local Ordinary of the Catholic partner, after having consulted the local Ordinary of the place where the marriage will be celebrated, may for grave reasons dispense the Catholic partner from the observance of the canonical form of marriage.[178]

----

175. Cf. C.I.C. 1127.2 and D.E. 150 Origins vol. 23 no. 9.

176. Cf. *Statement on the Implementation of the Apostolic Letter on Mixed Marriages no. 5-6.* N.C.C.B., November 16, 1970.

177. Cf. D.E. 177.

178. Cf. C.I.C. 1127.2; D.E. 150 Origins vol. 23 no. 9 and *Statement on the Implementation of the Apostolic Letter on Mixed Marriages no. 14-15.* N.C.C.B., November 16, 1970.

7. *The obligation imposed by some churches or ecclesial communities for the observance of their own form of marriage is not a motive for automatic dispensation from the Catholic canonical form. Such particular situations should form the subject of dialogue between the churches, at least at the local level.*[179]

8. What must be kept in mind is that if the wedding is celebrated with a dispensation from canonical form some public form of celebration is still required for validity. It is not permitted to have two separate religious services in which the exchange of consent would be expressed twice, or even one service which would celebrate two such exchanges of consent jointly or successively.[180]

9. *With the previous authorization of the local Ordinary, and if invited to do so, a Catholic priest or deacon may attend or participate in some way in the celebration of mixed marriages in situations where the dispensation from canonical form has been granted. In these cases there may be only one ceremony in which the presiding person receives the marriage vows. At the invitation of this celebrant, the Catholic priest or deacon may offer other appropriate prayers, read from the Scriptures, give a brief exhortation and bless the couple.*[181]

10. Upon request of the couple, the local Ordinary may permit the Catholic priest to invite the minister of the party of the other church or ecclesial community to participate in the celebration of the marriage, to read from the Scriptures (outside of the Nuptial Mass), give a brief exhortation and bless the couple.[182]

---

179. D.E. 155.

180. Cf. C.I.C. 1127.2 and D.E. 156.

181. D.E. 157.

182. Cf. D.E. 158 and *Statement on the Implementation of the Apostolic Letter on Mixed Marriages no. 14-15.* N.C.C.B., November 16, 1970.

11. *Because of problems concerning eucharistic sharing which may arise from the presence of non-Catholic witnesses and guests, a mixed marriage celebrated according to the Catholic form ordinarily takes place outside the eucharistic liturgy. For a just cause, however, the diocesan bishop may permit the celebration of the Eucharist. In the latter case, the decision as to whether the non-Catholic party of the marriage may be admitted to eucharistic communion is to be made in keeping with the general norms existing in the matter both for Eastern Christians and for other Christians, taking into account the particular situation of the reception of the sacrament of Christian marriage by two baptized Christians.*[183]

12. *Although the spouses in a mixed marriage share the sacraments of baptism and marriage, eucharistic sharing can only be exceptional and in each case the norms stated above concerning the admission of a non-Catholic Christian to eucharistic communion, as well as those concerning the participation of a Catholic in eucharistic communion in another church, must be observed.*[184]

---

183. D.E. 159.
184. D.E. 160.

B. Pre-nuptial Inquiry

1. Those who intend to be married should normally inform their pastor six months before marriage, in order to enable him to help them prepare for the celebration according to the laws of the Church. Local diocesan policies may suggest a lesser or greater time. In special cases and with the permission of the local Ordinary, a wedding can be solemnized within a shorter period of time.

2. If the parties choose to be married in a parish other than their own, the pastor, who has received permission from the local Ordinary or from the pastor of the parties, may not preside over the marriage until he receives the necessary documents. It is recommended that the documents be transmitted from one parish to another within the same diocese through the diocesan Curia.

3. The pastor, with the canonical right to assist at marriages at his parish, also has the responsibility to see that the necessary marriage preparation and Pre-nuptial Inquiry are carried out correctly.[185] He may request the assistance of another priest or lay person, if the case so requires.

4. The purpose of the Pre-nuptial Inquiry is:
   - So that it is certain that the persons involved are freely giving their consent to marry and that there are no obstacles or impediments that will invalidate the marriage or make it illicit, according to Canon or Civil Law.[186]

---

185. Cf. *Faithful to each other forever*, N.C.C.B., 1989, p. 96.

186. Cf. *ibid.* p. 95.

- To ensure that the couple possesses an adequate understanding of Catholic teaching, particularly on the nature, ends and essential properties of the sacrament of Matrimony.

5. The priest shall put the questions to the parties separately, with due regard to their circumstances.

6. In inquiring about impediments, the priest shall briefly mention those that are likely to exist in the case at hand.

7. Finally, the priest shall inquire whether the parties are sufficiently instructed in Christian doctrine:

   - When one or both parties lack knowledge on the basic truths of our faith, they should be instructed during the interval before the wedding, so that they can comply with their duty of being the first catechists of their children.

   - All prospective contracting parties should participate in a pre-Cana Seminar, a Catholic Marriage Preparation Course, or an equivalent to these classes.

8. A baptismal certificate, issued within six months of the marriage shall always be required from both parties. Whenever the baptismal certificate cannot be obtained, sworn statements will suffice.

9. Widows and widowers shall be required to present authentic certificates of the death of their departed spouses.

10. Special care and precautions should be taken in the case of persons whose previous marriage has been declared null and void by the Catholic Church. They shall be required to submit authentic Church documents regarding their freedom to marry, besides their baptismal certificate.

11. Extreme caution is needed in cases of divorced persons. Their civil and canonical freedom to marry is to be established before they are admitted to a canonical wedding.

12. Publication of the banns—in the dioceses that it is required—may also be done in another parish or parishes where there exists a reasonable suspicion that one or both parties might have incurred a matrimonial impediment.

C. Preparation for Confession

"To those who have been far away from the sacrament of Reconciliation and forgiving love I make this appeal: come back to this source of grace; do not be afraid! Christ himself is waiting for you. He will heal you, and you will be at peace with God!"[187]

Carefully prepare for Confession before receiving the sacrament of Matrimony. Confession is an excellent opportunity for the future spouses to begin again a new life and to receive all the necessary graces for a successful marriage. A general Confession is advisable for all the sins of the past life, especially in the cases in which the last good Confession may have been years previous to the marriage.

The basic requirement for a good Confession is to have the intention of returning to God like the prodigal son[188] and to acknowledge our sins with true sorrow before his representative, the priest.[189] Many couples have found that this sacrament, in addition to its spiritual benefit, has enabled them to approach their marriage more joyfully.

I. EXAMINATION OF CONSCIENCE [190]

Examine your conscience. Recall your sins. Calmly ask yourself what you have done with full knowledge and full consent against God's Commandments. The list that follows is not meant to intimidate prospective penitents. It is necessary to be thorough and demanding with oneself. If it has been a long time since the sacrament was approached, you may want to meet more than once with the priest. Do not be afraid to seek his advice with the confidence that

---

187. *Homily of John Paul II on September 13, 1987* at Westover Hills, San Antonio, Texas.

188. Cf. *Luke 15:17-19*.

189. Cf. *John 20:23*.

190. James P. Socías. *Handbook of Prayers.* (Chicago, IL: Midwest Theological Forum, 1993), pp. 323-334.

even though your sins may be serious and many, with true sorrow, Our Lord always forgives.

THE FIRST COMMANDMENT

- Have I performed my duties towards God reluctantly or grudgingly?
- Did I recite my usual prayers?
- Did I receive Holy Communion in the state of mortal sin or without the necessary preparation?
- Did I fail to keep the one-hour Eucharistic fast?
- Did I fail to mention some grave sin in my previous confessions?
- Did I seriously believe in superstition or engage in superstitious practices (fortune-telling, horoscopes, palm-reading, etc.)?
- Did I seriously doubt in matters of Faith? Did I put my Faith in danger by reading books, pamphlets, or magazines which contain errors or are contrary to Catholic faith and morals?
- Did I endanger my Faith by joining or attending meetings and activities of organizations contrary to the Church or to the Catholic faith (non-Catholic prayer-meetings, the Communist Party, Freemasonry, "weird" cults and other religions)?
- Have I committed the sin of sacrilege (profanation of a sacred person, place or thing)?

THE SECOND COMMANDMENT

- Did I try my best to fulfill the promises and resolutions which I made to God?
- Did I take the name of God in vain? Did I make use of God's name mockingly, jokingly, angrily or in any other irreverent manner?
- Did I make use of the Blessed Virgin Mary's name or the saints names mockingly, jokingly, angrily or in any other irreverent manner?

- Have I been a sponsor in baptism and ceremonies outside the Catholic Church?
- Did I tell a lie under oath?
- Did I break (private or public) vows?

THE THIRD COMMANDMENT

- Did I miss Mass on Sundays or Holy Days of obligation?
- Did I allow myself to be distracted during Mass?
- Have I arrived at Mass so late without sufficient reason that I failed to fulfill the Sunday obligation?
- Did I generously help the Church to the extent that I am able?
- Did I fast and abstain on the days prescribed by the Church?
- Have I done any work or business that would inhibit the worship due to God, the joy proper to the Lord's Day, or the appropriate relaxation of mind and body, on Sundays and Holy Days of obligation?

THE FOURTH COMMANDMENT

- Have I neglected to help my family in their needs?
- Have I been disobedient towards my parents?
- Did I treat my parents with little affection or respect?
- Did I quarrel with my brothers and sisters?

THE FIFTH COMMANDMENT

- Did I easily get angry or lose my temper?
- Was I envious or jealous of others?
- Did I injure or take the life of anyone? Was I ever reckless in driving?
- Was I an occasion for others to sin with my conversations, jokes, way of dressing, invitations to attend certain shows, lending them harmful books or maga-

zines, helping them to steal, etc.? Did I try to repair the harm done?

- Did I lead any person to sin? What sins?
- Did I neglect my health? Did I ever attempt to take my life?
- Did I get drunk or take prohibited drugs?
- Did I eat or drink in excess, allowing myself to get carried away by gluttony?
- Did I participate in any form of physical violence?
- Did I consent or actively take part in direct sterilization ("tubal ligation," vasectomy, etc.)?
- Did I consent, recommend, advise, or actively take part in an abortion? Am I aware that the Church punishes with excommunication those who procure and achieve abortion? Do I realize that this is a very grave crime?
- Did I cause anyone harm with my words or actions?
- If someone has offended me, have I desired revenge, harbor enmity, hatred or ill-feelings?
- Did I ask pardon whenever I offended anyone?
- Did I insult or offfend others?

The Sixth and Ninth Commandments

- Did I entertain indecent thoughts?
- Did I recall impure thoughts?
- Did I consent to evil desires against chastity, even though I may not have carried them out? Were there any circumstances which aggravated the sin (e.g. the affinity with, the married state or the consecration to God of the person involved)?
- Did I engage in impure conversations?
- Did I look for forms of entertainment which put me in proximate occasions of sin (some dances, immoral movies or shows, readings, bad company)?

- Do I realize that I may already be committing a sin by putting myself in occasions of sin (sharing a room with a person of the opposite sex, being alone with a person of the opposite sex in ways that could lead to sin, etc.)?
- Do I take care of those details of modesty and decency which are the safeguards of purity?
- Did I willfully look at immodest pictures or cast immodest looks upon myself or others? Did I willfully desire to commit such sins?
- Did I commit impure acts? By myself through the practice of self-abuse, which is a mortal sin? With someone else? How many times? With people of the same or opposite sex? Was there any circumstance of relationship, affinity, etc., which could have given the sin special gravity? Did these illicit relationships have any consequences? Did I do anything to prevent these consequences?
- Do I have friendships which are habitual occasions of sin? Am I prepared to break with them?
- In courtship, is true love my fundamental reason for dealing with the other person? Did I put the person I love in danger of sinning? Do I degrade human love by confusing it with selfishness or pleasure?
- Did I engage in acts such as "petting," "necking," passionate kisses or prolonged embraces?

The Seventh and Tenth Commandments

- Did I steal any object or amount of money? How much was it worth? Did I give it back; or at least, do I have the intention to do so?
- Have I done or caused damage to others' property? To what amount?
- Did I harm anyone by deception, fraud, or coercion in business contracts or transactions?
- Did I spend beyond my means? Do I spend too much

money unnecessarily because of whim, vanity or caprice?

- Do I give alms according to my capacity?
- Am I envious of my neighbor's goods?
- Did I neglect to pay my debts?
- Did I retain things found or stolen?
- Did I desire to steal?
- Am I diligent in my work and studies or do I give in to laziness or love of comfort?
- Was I greedy? Do I have an excessively materialistic view of life?

THE EIGHTH COMMANDMENT

- Did I tell lies? Did I repair any damage which may have resulted as a consequence of this?
- Have I unjustly accused others?
- Did I sin by detraction, that is, telling the faults of others without necessity?
- Did I sin by calumny, that is, telling derogatory lies about others?
- Did I judge others rashly or have suspected others falsely?
- Did I engage in gossip, back-biting, or tale-telling?
- Did I reveal secrets without due cause?

If you remember other serious sins besides those indicated here, mention them in your Confession.

Be truly sorry for your sins. True contrition for sin is the most important part of the sacrament. Foster true sorrow, bringing to mind that one unrepented mortal sin merits the loss of heaven and the pains of hell (imperfect contrition). Most of all be repentant for having offended your Father God, who sent his only Son, Jesus Christ to suffer and die for your sins (perfect contrition).

The *resolution to avoid committing these sins in the future* (purpose of amendment) is a sure sign that your sorrow is genuine and authentic. This does not mean that a guarantee and promise never to fall again into sin is necessary. A resolution to try to avoid the near occasions of sin suffices for true repentance. God's grace in cooperation with the intention to rectify your life will give you the strength to resist and overcome temptation in the future.

You are now prepared to make a good Confession.

II. DURING CONFESSION

You can begin your confession by making the sign of the cross. The priest gives you a blessing so that you make a good confession. You may respond by reciting a brief penitential prayer taken from Scripture. For example: "Lord, you know all things, you know that I love you" (Jn 21:17). You may also use the traditional opening, "Bless me Father, for I have sinned. My last good confession was . . . (how many weeks, months, or years approximately).

Say the sins that you remember. Start with the one that is most difficult to say. After this it will be easier to mention the rest. If you received general absolution, tell this to the priest and the sins forgiven then.

If you do not know how to confess or if you feel uneasy or ashamed, simply ask the priest to assist you. Be assured he will help you make a good confession. Simply answer the questions without hiding anything. As long as you do your best, God forgives all your sins, even if you forget to mention some.

If you do not remember any serious sins, be sure to confess at least some of your venial sins, adding at the end: "I am sorry for these and all the sins of my past life, especially for . . . (mention in general any past sin for which you are particularly sorry, for example all my sins against charity, purity, etc.)."

Listen to the advice the priest may give. After your confession of sins, the priest will give you personal encouragement and guidance to improve your Christian life.

Be willing to do the penance the priest gives you (some prayer or good work) to make reparation for your sins. This *penance* will diminish the temporal punishment due to sins already forgiven.

Say the Act of Contrition when the priest asks you to express your sorrow. You may do it in these or similar words:

O my God, I am heartily sorry for having offended you and I detest all my sins, because I dread the loss of heaven and the pains of hell; but most of all because they offend you, my God, who are all good and deserving of all my love. I firmly resolve with the help of your grace, to confess my sins, to do penance, and to amend my life. Amen.

or:

Lord Jesus, Son of God, have mercy on me, a sinner.

Afterwards the priest absolves you in these words: *I absolve you from your sins, in the name of the Father, and of the Son, and of the Holy Spirit.* Humbly listen to the absolution and respond, "Amen."

III. AFTER CONFESSION

Give thanks to your Savior for the grace of reconciliation just received.

Promptly and devoutly *fulfill the penance* given by the priest. Although you may receive Holy Communion even before performing your penance, it is advisable to perform it as soon as possible.

If you *recall some serious sin* you forgot to tell, rest assured that it has been forgiven with the others. But be sure to confess it in your next Confession.

RITE OF CONFESSION

After the customary greetings, the penitent makes the sign of the cross:

In the name of the Father, and of the Son, and of the Holy Spirit. Amen.

The priest urges the penitent to have confidence in God. The priest may say:

May the Lord be in your heart and help you to confess your sins with true sorrow.

Either the priest or the penitent may read or say by heart some words taken from the Holy Scripture about the mercy of God and repentance, e.g.:

Lord, you know all things; you know that I love you (John 21:17).

The penitent accuses himself of his sins. The priest gives the opportune advice, imposes the penance on him, and invites the penitent to manifest his contrition. The penitent may say for example:

Lord Jesus, Son of God, have mercy on me, a sinner.

The priest gives him the absolution:

God, the Father of mercies, through the death and resurrection of his Son, has reconciled the world to himself and sent the Holy Spirit among us for the forgiveness of sins; through the ministry of the Church, may God give you pardon and peace, and I absolve you from your sins in the name of the Father, and of the Son, and of the Holy Spirit.

The penitent answers: **Amen.**

The priest dismisses the penitent with this or any of the alternative formulae:

May the Passion of our Lord Jesus Christ, the intercession of the Blessed Virgin Mary and of all the saints, whatever good you do and suffering you endure, heal your sins, help you to grow in holiness, and reward you with eternal life. Go in peace.

The penitent should fulfill the penance imposed.

D. Formalities for the Celebration of Marriage

STEPS TO BE TAKEN BY THE FUTURE SPOUSES

SIX MONTHS BEFORE

I. Talk to the pastor of the parish where you wish the wedding to be celebrated (this is usually the parish of either the bride or the groom, although it is possible for another parish to be selected). Arrange with him who will be the priest (or deacon) that will preside over the marriage. Usually, the priest of the parish where the wedding will be celebrated officiates the marriage in the parish of either the bride or the groom.

II. You should visit:

A. Your own pastor and ask for the sacrament of confirmation if you have not received it previously.

B. The priest of the parish where the wedding ceremony is to take place (if it is not the parish either of the bride or the groom):

- To reserve the parish for a specific day and time.
- To make the appointment for the pre-nuptial inquiries. That interview should be done separately for each of the future spouses.
- To discuss with him what kind of preparation you will need for marriage:
  - Spiritual preparation as a top priority (frequent Confession and Communion, spiritual guidance, reading of appropriate books, etc.).
  - A premarital course organized by the Diocese is a common requirement established by the Bishops Conference. *Nevertheless, such preparation must always be set forth and put into practice in such a way*

> *that omitting it is not an impediment to the celebration of marriage.*[191]

- To coordinate the basic material arrangements regarding the Nuptial Mass.

OTHER FORMALITIES

1. Baptismal certificates from the parish where each one was baptized, less than six months old.

2. First Communion and Confirmation certificates may be requested.

3. A marriage license, according to state and local laws, must be submitted to the officiating priest (or deacon) before the ceremony.

4. For widows or widowers who want to remarry, an authentic death certificate of the husband or wife is needed.

5. You must submit the following before the ceremony:
   - Names of the witnesses.
   - If you wish wedding booklets to be used, submit the manuscript before they are printed.

6. You should also begin studying the liturgy of the wedding ceremony with your future spouse. You will also need to have a rehearsal in the parish where the wedding will be celebrated. The special witnesses can also be invited.

7. The publication of the banns will be made according to the particular regulations of each diocese.

8. It would be good to go to Confession some time before the wedding so you will receive the grace of the sacrament of Matrimony. This spiritual preparation helps to receive the special grace that comes with the sacrament of Matrimony.

---

191. F.C. 66.

E. THE WEDDING MASS

Whenever marriage is celebrated during Mass, white vestments are worn and the wedding Mass is used. If the marriage is celebrated on a Sunday or solemnity, the Mass of the day is used with the nuptial blessing and the special final blessing according to the circumstances.

The liturgy of the word as adapted to the marriage celebration, however, is a highly effective means for the catechesis on the sacrament of marriage and its duties. Therefore when the wedding Mass may not be held, one of the readings from the texts provided for the marriage celebration may be chosen, except from Holy Thursday to Easter, on the solemnities of Epiphany, Ascension, Pentecost, or Corpus Christi, or on Holy Days of obligation. On the Sundays of the Christmas season and in Ordinary Time, the entire wedding Mass may be used in Masses that are not parish Masses.

When a marriage is celebrated during Advent or Lent or other days of penance, the parish priest should advise the couple to take into consideration the special nature of these liturgical seasons.

(*Rite of Marriage*, "Introduction," no. 11)

WEDDING MASS

Rite for Celebrating Marriage during Mass

ENTRANCE RITE

At the appointed time, the priest, vested for Mass, goes with the ministers to the door of the church or, if more suitable, to the altar. There he meets the bride and bridegroom in a friendly manner, showing that the Church shares their joy.

Where it is desirable that the rite of welcome be omitted, the celebration of marriage begins at once with the Mass.

If there is a procession to the altar, the ministers go first, followed by the priest, and then the bride and the bridegroom. According to local custom, they may be escorted by at least their parents and the two witnesses. Meanwhile, the entrance song is sung..

If there is no singing for the entrance the following antiphon may be recited:

Entrance Antiphon   Ps 19: 3.5

May the Lord send you help from his holy place and from Zion may he watch over you. May he grant you your heart's desire and lend his aid to all your plans.

OPENING PRAYER

Father,
you have made the bond of marriage
a holy mystery,
a symbol of Christ's love for his Church.
Hear our prayers for N. and N.
With faith in you and in each other
they pledge their love today.
May their lives always bear witness
to the reality of that love.

We ask this through our Lord Jesus Christ, your Son,
who lives and reigns with you and the Holy Spirit,
one God, for ever and ever.

Almighty God,
hear our prayers for N. and N.,
who have come here today
to be united in the sacrament of marriage.
Increase their faith in you and in each other,
and through them bless your Church (with Christian
    children).

We ask this through our Lord Jesus Christ, your Son,
who lives and reigns with you and the Holy Spirit,
one God, for ever and ever.

or

Father,
hear our prayers for N. and N.,
who today are united in marriage before your altar.
Give them your blessing.
and strengthen their love for each other.

We ask this through our Lord Jesus Christ, your Son,
who lives and reigns with you and the Holy Spirit,
one God, for ever and ever.

or

Father,
when you created mankind
you willed that man and wife should be one.
Bind N. and N. in the loving union of marriage
and make their love fruitful
so that they may be living witnesses
to your divine love in the world.

We ask this through our Lord Jesus Christ, your Son,
who lives and reigns with you and the Holy Spirit,
one God, for ever and ever.

LITURGY OF THE WORD

The liturgy of the word is celebrated according to the rubrics. There may be three readings, the first of them from the Old Testament.

(The first two readings need not be done by a priest or deacon. Perhaps one of the parents of the bride and groom could each read one, or some members of the wedding party or other close friends. Some readings have a shorter form. This is indicated with a star * at the beginning. Only the portions between »» «« should be read when using the shorter form.)

After the gospel, the priest gives a homily drawn from the sacred text. He speaks about the mystery of Christian marriage, the dignity of wedded love, the grace of the sacrament and the responsibilities of married people, keeping in mind the circumstances of this particular marriage.

FIRST READING
(FROM THE OLD TESTAMENT)

B - 1   [774.1]

CREATION OF MAN AND WOMAN

A reading from the book of Genesis   1: 26-28. 31

Male and female he created them.

God said, 'Let us make man in our own image, in the likeness of ourselves, and let them be masters of the fish of the sea, the birds of heaven, the cattle, all the wild beasts and all the reptiles that crawl upon the earth.'

God created man in the image of himself,
in the image of God he created him,
male and female he created them.

God blessed them, saying to them, 'Be fruitful, multiply, fill the earth and conquer it. Be masters of the fish of the sea, the birds of heaven and all living animals on the earth.' God saw all he had made, and indeed it was very good.

The word of the Lord.

B - 2   [774.2]

INDISSOLUBILITY OF MARRIAGE

A reading from the book of Genesis   2: 18-24

And they became two in one flesh.

The Lord God said, 'It is not good that the man should be alone. I will make him a helpmate.' So from the soil the Lord God fashioned all the wild beasts and all the birds of heaven. These he brought to the man to see what he would call them; each one was to bear the name the man would give it. The man gave names to all the cattle, all the birds of heaven and all the wild beasts. But no helpmate suitable for man was found for him.

So the Lord God made the man fall into a deep sleep. And while he slept, he took one of his ribs and enclosed it in flesh. The Lord God built the rib he had taken from the man into a woman, and brought her to the man. The man exclaimed:

'This at last is bone from my bones,
and flesh from my flesh!
This is to be called woman,
for this was taken from man.'

This is why a man leaves his father and mother and joins himself to his wife, and they become one body.

The word of the Lord.

B - 3   [774.3]

MARRIAGE OF ISAAC AND REBEKAH

A reading from the book of Genesis   24: 48-51. 58-67

Isaac loved Rebekah and so he was consoled
for the loss of his mother

Abraham's servant said to Laban: 'I blessed the Lord, God of my master Abraham, who had so graciously led me to choose the daughter of my master's brother for his son. Now tell me whether you are prepared to show kindness and goodness to my master; if not, say so, and I shall know what to do.'

Laban and Bethuel replied, 'This is from the Lord; it is not in our power to say yes or no to you. Rebekah is there before you. Take her and go; and let her become the wife of your master's son, as the Lord has decreed.'

They called Rebekah and asked her, 'Do you want to leave with this man?' 'I do,' she replied. Accordingly they let their sister Rebekah go, with her nurse, and Abraham's servant and his men. They blessed Rebekah in these words:

'Sister of ours, increase to thousands
and tens of thousands!

May your descendants gain possession
of the gates of their enemies!'

Rebekah and her servants stood up, mounted the camels, and followed the man. The servant took Rebekah and departed.

Isaac, who lived in the Negeb, had meanwhile come into the wilderness of the well of Lahai Roi.

Now Isaac went walking in the fields as evening fell, and looking up saw camels approaching. And Rebekah looked up and saw Isaac. She jumped down from her camel, and asked the servant, 'Who is that man walking through the fields to meet us?' The servant replied, 'That is my master'; then she took her veil and hid her face. The servant told Isaac the whole story, and Isaac led Rebekah into his tent and made her his wife; and he loved her. And so Isaac was consoled for the loss of his mother.

The word of the Lord.

B - 4   [774.4]

MARRIAGE OF TOBIAS AND SARAH

A reading from the book of Tobit   7: 9-10. 11-17

May God join you together and fill you with his blessings.

Then Tobias said to Raphael, 'Brother Azarias, will you ask Raguel to give me my sister Sarah?'

Raguel overheard the words, and said to the young man, 'Eat and drink, and make the most of your evening; no one else has the right to take my daughter Sarah—no one but you, my brother. In any case I, for my own part, am not at liberty to give her to anyone else, since you are her next of kin. However, my boy, I must be frank with you: I have tried to find a husband for her seven times among our kinsmen, and all of them have died the first evening, on going to her room. But for the present, my boy, eat and drink; the Lord will grant you his grace and peace.' Tobias spoke out, 'I will not hear of eating and drinking till you have come to a decision about me.' Raguel answered, 'Very well. Since, as prescribed by the Book of Moses, she is given to you, heaven itself decrees she shall be yours. I shall therefore entrust your sister to you. From now you are her brother and she is your sister. She is given to you from today for ever. The Lord of heaven favour you tonight, my child, and grant you his grace and peace.' Raguel called for his daughter Sarah, took her by the hand and gave her to Tobias with these words, 'I entrust her to you; the law and the ruling recorded in the Book of Moses assign her to you as your wife. Take her; take her home to your father's house with a good conscience. The God of heaven grant you a good journey in peace.' Then he turned to her mother and asked her to fetch him writing paper. He drew up the marriage contract, how he gave his daughter as bride to Tobias according to the ordinance in the Law of Moses.

After this they began to eat and drink.

The word of the Lord.

B - 5   [774.5]

PRAYER OF TOBIAS AND SARAH

A reading from the book of Tobit   8:4-9

May God bring us to old age together.

On the evening of their marriage, Tobias said to Sarah, 'You and I must pray and petition our Lord to win his grace and protection.' They began praying for protection, and this was how he began:

'You are blessed, O God of our fathers;
blessed, too, is your name
for ever and ever.
Let the heavens bless you
and all things you have made
for evermore.

It was you who created Adam,
you who created Eve his wife
to be his help and support;
and from these two the human race was born.
It was you who said:

"It is not good that the man should be alone;
let us make him a helpmate like himself."
And so I do not take my sister
for any lustful motive;
I do it in singleness of heart.
Be kind enough to have pity on her and on me
and bring us to old age together."

And together they said, 'Amen, Amen'.

The word of the Lord.

B- 6

[774.6]

LOVE IS AS STRONG AS DEATH

A reading from the Song of Songs   2: 8-10. 14. 16; 8: 6-7

Love is as strong as death.

I hear my Beloved.
See how he comes
leaping on the mountains,
bounding over the hills.
My Beloved is like a gazelle,
like a young stag.
See where he stands
behind our wall.
He looks in at the window,
he peers through the lattice.

My Beloved lifts up his voice,
he says to me,
'Come then, my love,
my lovely one, come.
My dove hiding in the clefts of the rock.
In the coverts of the cliff,
show me your face,
let me hear your voice;
for your voice is sweet
and your face is beautiful.'

My beloved is mine and I am his.

Set me like a seal on your heart,
like a seal on your arm.
For love is as strong as Death
jealousy relentless as Sheol.
The flash of it is a flash of fire,
a flame of the Lord himself.
Love no flood can quench,
no torrents down.

The word of the Lord.

B - 7 [774.7]

THE GOOD WIFE

A reading from the book of Sirach   26: 1-4. 16-21

Like the sun rising is the beauty of a good wife in a well-kept house.

Happy the husband of a really good wife;
the number of his days will be doubled.
A perfect wife is the joy of her husband,
he will live out the years of his life in peace.
A good wife is the best of portions,
reserved for those who fear the Lord;
rich or poor, they will be glad of heart,
cheerful of face, whatever the season.
The grace of a wife will charm her husband,
her accomplishments will make him stronger.

A silent wife is a gift from the Lord,
no price can be put on a well-trained character.
A modest wife is a boon twice over,
a chaste character cannot be weighed on scales.
Like the sun rising over the mountains of the Lord
is the beauty of a good wife in a well-kept house.

The word of the Lord.

B - 8   [774.8]

THE NEW COVENANT MADE BY GOD

A reading from the book of Jeremiah   Jer 31: 31-32. 33-34

I will make a new covenant with the House of Israel
and the House of Judah.

See, the days are coming—it is the Lord who speaks—when
I will make a new covenant with the House of Israel and the
House of Judah, but not a covenant like the one I made with
their ancestors on the day I took them by the hand to bring
them out of the land of Egypt. No, this is the covenant I will
make with the House of Israel when those days arrive—it is
the Lord who speaks. Deep within them I will plant my Law,
writing it on their hearts. Then I will be their God and they
shall be my people. There will be no further need for neighbour
to try to teach neighbour, or brother to say to brother, 'Learn to
know the Lord!' No, they will all know me, the least no less
than the greatest—it is the Lord who speaks.

The word of the Lord.

RESPONSORIAL PSALM

 [776.1]

HYMN TO THE PROVIDENCE OF THE LORD

cf. Ps 33: 12. 18. 20-21, 22

R. The earth is full of the goodness of the Lord.

Happy the nation whose God is Yahweh,
the people he has chosen for his heritage.
But see how the eye of Yahweh is on
   those who fear him,
on those who rely on his love. **R.**

Our soul awaits Yahweh,
he is our help and shield;
our hearts rejoice in him,
we trust in his holy name. **R.**

Yahweh, let your love rest on us
as our hope has rested in you. **R.**

C- 2   [776.2]

PRAISING THE JUSTICE OF GOD

cf. Ps 34: 2-3, 4-5, 6-7, 8-9

R. I will bless the Lord at all times
or: **R.** Taste and see the goodness of the Lord

My soul glories in Yahweh,
let the humble hear and rejoice.
Proclaim with me the greatness of Yahweh,
together let us extol his name. **R.**

I seek Yahweh, and he answers me
and frees me from all my fears
Every face turned to him grows brighter
and is never ashamed. **R.**

A cry goes up from the poor man, and Yahweh hears,
and helps him in all his troubles.
The angel of Yahweh pitches camp round
  those who fear him;
  and he keeps them safe. **R.**

How good Yahweh is—only taste and see!
Happy the man who takes shelter in him.
Fear Yahweh, you his holy ones:
those who fear him want for nothing. **R.**

C- 3   [776.3]

GOD IS LOVE

cf. Ps 103: 1-2, 8. 13. 17-18a

R. The Lord is kind and merciful.

or: **R.** The Lord's kindness is everlastlng
     to those who fear him.

Bless Yahweh, my soul,
bless his holy name, all that is in me!
Bless Yahweh, my soul,
and remember all his kindnesses. **R.**

Yahweh is tender and compassionate,
slow to anger, most loving.
As tenderly as a father treats his children,
so Yahweh treats those who fear him. **R.**

Yet Yahweh's love for those who fear him
lasts trom all eternity and for ever,
like his goodness to their children's children,
as long as they keep his covenant. **R.**

[776.4]

HAPPY ARE THOSE WHO OBEY THE LORD

cf. Ps 112: 12, 3-4, 5-7a, 7bc-8, 9

R. Happy are those who do what the Lord commands.

or: **R.**   Alleluia.

Happy the man who fears Yahweh
by joyfully keeping his commandments!
Children of such a man will be powers on earth,
descendants of the upright will always be blessed. **R.**

There will be riches and wealth for his family
and his righteousness can never change.
For the upright he shines like a lamp in the dark,
he is merciful, tenderhearted, virtuous. **R.**

Interest is not charged by this good man,
he is honest in all his dealings.
Kept safe by virtue, he is ever steadfast,
and leaves an imperishable memory behind him;
with constant heart, and confidence in Yahweh. **R.**

He need never fear bad news.
Steadfast in heart he overcomes his fears:
in the end he will triumph over his enemies. **R.**

Quick to be generous, he gives to the poor,
his righteousness can never change,
men such as this will always be honored. **R.**

[776.5]

HAPPY ARE THOSE WHO FEAR THE LORD

cf. Ps 128: 1-2, 3, 4-5

R. Happy are those who fear the Lord.

or: **R.** See how the Lord blesses those who fear him.

Happy, all those who fear Yahweh
and follow in his paths.
You will eat what your hands have worked for,
happiness and prosperity will be yours.   **R.**

Your wife: a fruitful vine
on the inner walls of your house.
Your sons: round your table
like shoots round an olive tree.   **R.**

Such are the blessings that fall
on the man who fears Yahweh.
May Yahweh bless you from Zion
all the days of your life!   **R.**

C - 6   [776.6]

THE LORD IS MERCIFUL AND COMPASSIONATE

cf. Ps 145: 8-9, 10 and 15,17-18

R. The Lord is compassionate to all his creatures.

He, Yahweh, is merciful, tenderhearted,
slow to anger very loving,
and universally kind;
Yahweh's tenderness embraces all his creatures.   **R.**

Yahweh, all your creatures thank you,
and your faithful bless you.
Patiently all creatures look to you
to feed them throughout the year.   **R.**

Righteous in all that he does,
Yahweh acts only out of love,
standing close to all who invoke him,
close to all who invoke Yahweh faithfully.   **R.**

[776.7]

HYMN OF THANKSGIVING

cf. Ps 148: 1-2, 3-4, 9-10,11-12ab, 12c-14a

R. Let all praise the name of the Lord.

or: **R.** Alleluia.

Let heaven praise Yahweh:
praise him, heavenly heights,
praise him, all his angels, praise him, all his armies! **R.**

Praise him, sun and moon,
praise him, shining stars, praise him, highest heavens,
and waters above the heavens! **R.**

Mountains and hills,
orchards and forests,
wild animals and farm animals,
snakes and birds. **R.**

All kings on earth and nations,
princes, all rulers in the world,
young men and girls,
old people, and children too! **R.**

Let them all praise the name of Yahweh,
for his name and no other is sublime,
transcending earth and heaven in majesty,
raising the fortunes of his people. **R.**

SECOND READING
(FROM THE NEW TESTAMENT)

D-1   [775.1]

NOTHING CAN SEPARATE US FROM
THE LOVE OF CHRIST

A reading from the letter of Paul
to the Romans   8: 31b-35. 37-39

Who will separate us from the love of Christ?

With God on our side who can be against us? Since God did not spare his own Son, but gave him up to benefit us all, we may be certain, after such a gift, that he will not refuse anything he can give. Could anyone accuse those that God has chosen? When God acquits, could anyone condemn? Could Christ Jesus? No! He not only died for us—he rose from the dead, and there at God's right hand he stands and pleads for us.

Nothing therefore can come between us and the love of Christ, even if we are troubled or worried, or being persecuted, or lacking food or clothes, or being threatened or even attacked. As scripture promised: For your sake we are being massacred daily, and reckoned as sheep for the slaughter. These are the trials through which we triumph, by the power of him who loved us.

For I am certain of this: neither death nor life, no angel, no prince, nothing that exists, nothing still to come, not any power, or height or depth, nor any created thing, can ever come between us and the love of god made visible in Christ Jesus our Lord.

The word of the Lord.

D - 2 [775.2]

OFFER YOUR LIVING BODIES TO GOD
AS A HOLY SACRIFICE

A reading from the letter of Paul
to the Romans 12: 1-2, 9-18

Offer to God your bodies as a living and holy sacrifice,
truly pleasing to him.

»»Think of God's mercy, my brothers, and worship him, I beg you, in a way that is worthy of thinking beings, by offering your living bodies as a holy sacrifice, truly pleasing to God. Do not model yourselves on the behaviour of the world around you, but let your behaviour change, modelled by your new mind. This is the only way to discover the will of God and know what is good what it is that God wants, what is the perfect thing to do.

Do not let your love be a pretence, but sincerely prefer good to evil. Love each other as much as brothers should, and have a profound respect for each other. Work for the Lord with untiring effort and with great earnestness of spirit. If you have hope, this will make you cheerful. Do not give up if trials come; and keep on praying. If any of the saints are in need you must share with them; and you should make hospitality your special care.««

Bless those who persecute you: never curse them, bless them. Rejoice with those who rejoice and be sad with those in sorrow. Treat everyone with equal kindness; never be condescending but make real friends with the poor. Do not allow yourself to become self-satisfied. Never repay evil with evil but let everyone see that you are interested only in the highest ideals. Do all you can to live at peace with everyone.

The word of the Lord.

D -3

[775.3]

YOUR BODY IS A TEMPLE OF THE HOLY SPIRIT

A reading from the first letter of St. Paul
to the Corinthians   6:13c-15a. 17-20

Your body is a temple of the Spirit.

The body is not meant for fornication; it is for the Lord, and the Lord for the body. God who raised the Lord from the dead, will by his power raise us up too.

You know, surely, that your bodies are members making up the body of Christ; anyone who is joined to the Lord is one spirit with him.

Keep away from fornication. All the other sins are committed outside the body; but to fornicate is to sin against your own body. Your body, you know, is the temple of the Holy Spirit, who is in you since you received him from God. You are not your own property; you have been bought—and paid for. That is why you should use your body for the glory of God.

The word of the Lord.

[775.4]

LOVE IS ABOVE ALL VIRTUES

A reading from the first letter of Paul
to the Corinthians   12: 31- 13: 8

If I am without love, it will do me no good whatever.

Be ambitious for the higher gifts. And I am going to show you a way that is better than any of them.

If I have all the eloquence of men or of angels, but speak without love, I am simply a gong booming or a cymbal clashing. If I have the gift of prophecy, understanding all the mysteries there are, and knowing everything, and if I have faith in all its fulness, to move mountains, but without love, then I am nothing at all. If I give away all that I possess, piece by piece, and if I even let them take my body to burn it, but am without love, it will do me no good whatever.

Love is always patient and kind; it is never jealous; love is never boastful or conceited; it is never rude or selfish; it does not take offence, and is not resentful. Love takes no pleasure in other people's sins but delights in the truth; it is always ready to excuse, to trust, to hope, and to endure whatever comes.

Love does not come to an end.

The word of the Lord.

[775.5]

MARRIAGE IS IMAGE OF THE UNION
BETWEEN CHRIST AND HIS CHURCH

A reading from the letter of Paul
to the Ephesians   5: 2. 21-33

This mystery has many implications and I am saying
it applies to Christ and the Church.

»»Follow Christ by loving as he loved you, giving himself up
in our place.«« Give way to one another in obedience to Christ.
Wives should regard their husbands as they regard the Lord,
since as Christ is head of the Church and saves the whole body,
so is a husband the head of his wife; and as the Church submits
to Christ, so should wives to their husbands, in everything.
»»Husbands should love their wives just as Christ loved the
Church and sacrificed himself for her to make her holy. He
made her clean by washing her in water with a form of words,
so that when he took her to himself she would be glorious, with
no speck or wrinkle or anything like that, but holy and fault-
less. In the same way, husbands must love their wives as they
love their own bodies; for a man to love his wife is for him to
love himself. A man never hates his own body, but he feeds it
and looks after it; and that is the way Christ treats the Church,
because it is his body—and we are its living parts. For this
reason, a man must leave his father and mother and be joined
to his wife, and the two will become one body. This mystery
has many implications; but I am saying it applies to Christ and
the Church.«« To sum up; you too, each one of you, must love
his wife as he loves himself; and let every wife respect her
husband.

The word of the Lord.

D - 6   [775.6]

LOVE IS THE BOND OF PERFECTION

A reading from the letter of Paul
to the Colossians   3: 12-17

Above all have love, which is the bond of perfection.

You are God's chosen race, his saints; he loves you, and you should be clothed in sincere compassion, in kindness and humility, gentleness and patience. Bear with one another; forgive each other as soon as a quarrel begins. The Lord has forgiven you; now you must do the same. Over all these clothes, to keep them together and complete them, put on love. And may the peace of Christ reign in your hearts, because it is for this that you were called together as parts of one body. Always be thankful.

Let the message of Christ, in all its richness, find a home with you. Teach each other, and advise each other, in all wisdom. With gratitude in your hearts sing psalms and Hymns and inspired songs to God; and never say or do anything except in the name of the Lord Jesus, giving thanks to God the Father through him.

The word of the Lord.

D - 7   [775.7]

CHRISTIAN FRATERNITY

A reading from the first letter of Peter   3: 1-9

*You should all agree among yourselves
and be sympathetic, and love the brothers.*

Wives should be obedient to their husbands. Then, if there are some husbands who have not yet obeyed the word, they may find themselves won over, without a word spoken, by the way their wives behave, when they see how faithful and conscientious they are. Do not dress up for show: doing up your hair, wearing gold bracelets and fine clothes; all this should be inside, in a person's heart, imperishable: the ornament of a sweet and gentle disposition—this is what is precious in the sight of God. That was how the holy women of the past dressed themselves attractively—they hoped in God and were tender and obedient to their husbands; like Sarah, who was obedient to Abraham, and called him her lord. You are now her children, as long as you live good lives and do not give way to fear or worry.

In the same way, husbands must always treat their wives with consideration in their life together, respecting a woman as one who, though she may be the weaker partner, is equally an heir to the life of grace. This will stop anything from coming in the way of your prayers.

Finally: you should all agree among yourselves and be sympathetic; love the brothers, have compassion and be self-effacing. Never pay back one wrong with another one; instead, pay back with a blessing. That is what you are called to do, so that you inherit a blessing yourself.

The word of the Lord.

D - 8 [775.8]

LOVE ONE ANOTHER AS CHRIST TOLD US

A reading from the first letter of John   I Jn 3: 18-24

Our love is to be something real and active.

My children,
our love is not to be just words or mere talk,
but something real and active;
only by this can we be certain
that we are the children of the truth
and be able to quieten our conscience in his presence,
whatever accusations it may raise against us,
because God is greater than our conscience
        and he knows everything.
My dear people,
if we cannot be condemned by our own conscience,
we need not be afraid in God's presence,
and whatever we ask him,
we shall receive,
because we keep his commandments
and live the kind of life that he wants.
His commandments are these:
that we believe in the name of his Son Jesus Christ
and that we love one another
as he told us to.
Whoever keeps his commandments
lives in God and God lives in him.
We know that he lives in us
by the Spirit that he has given us.

    The word of the Lord.

D - 9   [775.9]

LOVE COMES FROM GOD

A reading from the first letter of John   I Jn 4: 7-12

God is love.

My dear people,
let us love one another
since love comes from God
and everyone who loves is begotten by God and knows God.
Anyone who fails to love can never have known God,
because God is love.
God's love for us was revealed
when God sent into the world his only Son
so that we could have life through him;
this is the love I mean:
not our love for God,
but God's love for us when he sent his Son
to be the sacrifice that takes our sins away.
My dear people,
since God has loved us so much,
we too should love one another.
No one has ever seen God;
but as long as we love one another
God will live in us
and his love will be complete in us.

The word of the Lord.

_____

D - 10 [775.2]

In the Easter Season

WEDDING FEAST OF THE LAMB

A reading from the book of Revelation 19: 1, 5-9a

Happy are those who are invited to the wedding feast of the Lamb.

Here is the message of the Amen, the faithful, the true witness, the ultimate source of God's creation: 'Look, I am standing at the door, knocking. If one of you hears me calling and opens the door, I will come in to share his meal, side by side with him. Those who prove victorious I will allow to share my throne, just as I was victorious myself and took my place with my Father on his throne. If anyone has ears to hear, let him listen to what the Spirit is saying to the churches.'

The word of the Lord.

ACCLAMATION
AND VERSE BEFORE THE GOSPEL

`E - 1`   [777.1]

I Jn 4: 8 and 11

R. **Alleluia.** God is love;
let us love one another as he has loved us. **R. Alleluia.**

`E - 2`   [777.2]

I Jn 4: 12

R. **Alleluia.** If we love one another
God will live in us in perfect love. **R. Alleluia.**

`E - 3`   [777.3]

I Jn 4: 16

R. **Alleluia.** He who lives in love, lives in God,
and God in him. **R. Alleluia.**

`E - 4`   [777.4]

I Jn 4: 7b

R. **Alleluia.** Everyone who loves is born of God
and knows him. **R. Alleluia.**

GOSPEL

 [778.1]

THE BEATITUDES

A reading from the holy Gospel
according to Matthew   5: 1-12

Rejoice and be glad, for your reward will be great in heaven.

Seeing the crowds, Jesus went up the hill. There he sat down and was joined by his disciples. Then he began to speak. This is what he taught them:

'How happy are the poor in spirit:
theirs is the kingdom of heaven.
Happy the gentle:
they shall have the earth for their heritage.
Happy those who mourn:
they shall be comforted.
Happy, those who hunger and thirst for what is right:
they shall be satisfied.
Happy the merciful:
they shall have mercy shown them.
Happy the pure in heart:
they shall see God.
Happy the peacemakers:
they shall be called sons of God.
Happy those who are persecuted in the cause of right:
theirs is the kingdom of heaven.

'Happy are you when people abuse you and persecute you and speak all kinds of calumny against you on my account. Rejoice and be glad, for your reward will be great in heaven.'

The Gospel of the Lord.

F - 2   [778.2]

CHIRSTIANS ARE THE SALT OF THE EARTH
AND THE LIGHT OF THE WORLD

A reading from the holy Gospel
according to Matthew   5: 13-16

You are the light of the world.

Jesus said to his disciples: 'You are the salt of the earth. But if salt becomes tasteless, what can make it salty again? It is good for nothing, and can only be thrown out to be trampled underfoot by men.

'You are the light of the world. A city built on a hill-top cannot be hidden. No one lights a lamp to put it under a tub; they put it on the lamp-stand where it shines for everyone in the house. In the same way your light must shine in the sight of men, so that, seeing your good works, they may give the praise to your Father in heaven.'

The Gospel of the Lord.

F - 3   [778.3]

DOING THE WILL OF GOD

A reading from the holy Gospel
according to Matthew   7: 21. 24-29

He built his house on rock.

Jesus said to his disciples:

»»'It is not those who say to me, "Lord, Lord," who will enter
the kingdom of heaven, but the person who does the will of my
Father in heaven.

Therefore, everyone who listens to these words of mine and
acts on them will be like a sensible man who built his house on
rock. Rain came down, floods rose, gales blew and hurled themselves against that house, and it did not fall: it was founded on
rock.«« But everyone who listens to these words of mine and
does not act on them will be like a stupid man who built his
house on sand. Rain came down, floods rose, gales blew and
struck that house, and it fell; and what a fall it had!'

Jesus had now finished what he wanted to say, and his teaching made a deep impression on the people because he taught
them with authority, and not like their own scribes.

The Gospel of the Lord.

———————————————

D - 4   [778.4]

INDISSOLUBILITY OF MARRIAGE

A reading from the holy Gospel
according to Matthew   19: 3-6

What God has united, man must not divide.

Some Pharisees approached Jesus, and to test him they said, 'Is
it against the Law for a man to divorce his wife on any pretext
whatever?' He answered, 'Have you not read that the creator
from the beginning made them male and female and that he
said: This is why a man must leave father and mother, and cling
to his wife, and the two become one body? They are no longer
two, therefore, but one body. So then, what God has united,
man must not divide.'

The Gospel of the Lord.

D - 5   [778.5]

LOVE IS THE GREATEST COMMANDMENT

A reading from the holy Gospel
according to Matthew   22: 35-40

This is the greatest and the first commandment.
The second is similar to it.

A lawyer, to disconcert Jesus, put a question, 'Master, which is the greatest commandment of the Law?' Jesus said, 'You must love the Lord your God with all your heart, with all your soul, and with all your mind. This is the greatest and the first commandment. The second resembles it: you must love your neighbor as yourself. On these two commandments hang the whole Law, and the Prophets also.'

The Gospel of the Lord.

F - 6   [778.6]

UNITY OF MARRIAGE

A reading from the holy Gospel
according to Mark   10: 6-9

They are no longer two, therefore, but one body.

Jesus said, 'From the beginning of creation God made them male
and female. This is why a man must leave father and mother,
and the two become one body. They are no longer two, therefore, but one body. So then, what God has united, man must
not divide.'

The Gospel of the Lord.

F - 7   [778.7]

WEDDING FEAST AT CANA

A reading from the holy Gospel
according to John   2: 1-11

This was the first of the signs given by Jesus - at Cana in Galilee.

There was a wedding at Cana in Galilee. The mother of Jesus was there, and Jesus and his disciples had also been invited. When they ran out of wine, since the wine provided for the wedding was all finished, the mother of Jesus said to him, "They have no wine." Jesus said, "Woman why turn to me? My hour has not come yet." His mother said to the servants, "Do whatever he tells you." There were six stone water jars standing there, meant for the ablutions that are customary among the Jews: each could hold twenty or thirty gallons. Jesus said to the servants, "Fill the jars with water," and they filled them to the brim. "Draw some out now," he told them, "and take it to the steward." They did this; the steward tasted the water, and it had turned into wine. Having no idea where it came from— only the servants who had drawn the water knew—the steward called the bridegroom and said, "People generally serve the best wine first, and keep the cheaper sort till the guests have had plenty to drink; but you have kept the best wine till now."

This was the first of the signs given by Jesus: it was given at Cana in Galilee.

He let his glory be seen and his disciples believed in him.

The Gospel of the Lord.

D - 8   [778.8]

LOVE ONE ANOTHER AS I LOVED YOU

A reading from the holy Gospel
according to John   15: 9-12

Remain in my love.

Jesus said to his disciples:

'As the Father has loved me,
so I have loved you.
Remain in my love.
If you keep my commandments
you will remain in my love,
just as I have kept my Father's commandments
and remain in his love.
I have told you this
so that my own joy may be in you
and your joy be complete.
This is my commandment:
love one another,
as I loved you.

The Gospel of the Lord.

D - 9 [778.9]

THE COMMANDMENT OF LOVE

A reading from the holy Gospel
according to John 15: 12-16

This is my commandment: love one another.

Jesus said to his disciples:

"This is my commandment:
love one another
as I have loved you.
A man can have no greater love for his friends.
You are my friends,
if you do what I command you.
I shall not call you servants any more,
because a servant does not know
his master's business;
I call you friends,
because I have made known to you
everything I have learnt from my Father.
You did not choose me,
no, I chose you;
and I commissioned you
to go out and to bear fruit,
fruit that will last;
and then the Father will give you
anything you ask him in my name."

The Gospel of the Lord.

D - 10 [778.10]

THE MYSTICAL BODY

A reading from the holy Gospel
according to John 17: 20-26

May they be completely one.

Jesus raised his eyes to heaven and said:

»»'Holy Father,
I pray not only for these,
but for those also
who through their words will believe in me.
May they all be one.
Father, may they be one in us
as you are in me and I am in you,
so that the world may believe it was you who sent me.
I have given them the glory you gave to me,
that they may be one as we are one.
With me in them and you in me,
may they be so completely one
that the world will realise that it was you who sent me
and that I have loved them as much as you love me.
Father,
I want those you have given me
to be with me where I am,
so that they may always see the glory
you have given me because you loved me ««
before the foundation of the world.
Father, Righteous One,
the world has not known you,
but I have known you,
and these have known
that you have sent me.
I have made your name known to them
and will continue to make it known,
so that the love with which you loved me may be in them,
and so that I may be in them.'

The Gospel of the Lord.

RITE OF MARRIAGE

INTRODUCTION

All stand, including the bride and bridegroom, and the priest addresses them in these or similar words:

My dear friends, you have come together in this church so that the Lord may seal and strengthen your love in the presence of the Church's minister and this community. Christ abundantly blesses this love. He has already consecrated you in baptism and now he enriches and strengthens you by a special sacrament so that you may assume the duties of marriage in mutual and lasting fidelity. And so, in the presence of the Church, I ask you to state your intentions.

QUESTIONS

The priest then questions them about their freedom of choice, faithfulness to each other, and the acceptance and upbringing of children:

N. and N., have you come here freely and without reservation to give yourselves to each other in marriage?

Will you love and honor each other as man and wife for the rest of your lives?

The following question may be omitted if, for example, the couple is advanced in years.

Will you accept children lovingly from God, and bring them up according to the law of Christ and his Church?

Each answers the questions separately.

CONSENT

The priest invites the couple to declare their consent:

Since it is your intention to enter into marriage, join your right hands, and declare your consent before God and his Church.

They join hands. The bridegroom says:

I, N., take you, N., to be my wife. I promise to be true to you in good times and in bad, in sickness and in health. I will love you and honor you all the days of my life.

The bride says:

I, N., take you, N., to be my husband. I promise to be true to you in good times and in bad, in sickness and in health. I will love you and honor you all the days of my life.

ALTERNATIVE CONSENT

If, however, it seems preferable for pastoral reasons, the priest may obtain consent from the couple through questions.

First he asks the bridegroom:

N., do you take N. to be your wife? Do you promise to be true to her in good times and in bad, in sickness and in health, to love her and honor her all the days of your life?

The bridegroom:

I do.

Then he asks the bride:

N., do you take N. to be your husband? Do you promise to be true to him in good times and in bad, in sickness and in health, to love him and honor him all the days of your life?

The bride:

I do.

ALTERNATIVE CONSENTS

In the dioceses of the United States, the following form may also be used:

I, N., take you, N., for my lawful wife, to have and to hold, from this day forward, for better, for worse, for richer, for poorer, in sickness and in health, until death do us part.

I, N., take you, N., for my lawful husband, to have and to hold, from this day forward, for better, for worse, for richer, for poorer, in sickness and in health, until death do us part.

If it seems preferable for pastoral reasons for the priest to obtain consent from the couple through questions, in the dioceses of the United States the following alternative form may be used:

N., do you take N. for your lawful wife (husband), to have and to hold, from this day forward, for better, for worse, for richer, for poorer, in sickness and in health, until death do you part?

The bride (bridegroom):

I do.

Receiving their consent, the priest says:

You have declared your consent before the Church.
May the Lord in his goodness strengthen your consent
and fill you both with his blessings.
What God has joined, men must not divide.

R. Amen.

BLESSING OF RINGS

Priest:

May the Lord bless + these rings
which you give to each other
as the sign of your love and fidelity.

R. Amen.

ALTERNATIVE BLESSINGS

Lord, bless these rings which we bless + in your name.
Grant that those who wear them
may always have a deep faith in each other.
May they do your will
and always live together
in peace, good will, and love.
We ask this through Christ our Lord.

R. Amen.

or:

Lord,
bless + and consecrate N. and N.
in their love for each other.
May these rings be a symbol
of true faith in each other,
and always remind them of their love.
We ask this through Christ our Lord.

R. Amen.

EXCHANGE OF RINGS

The bridegroom places his wife's ring on her ring finger. He may say:

N., take this ring as a sign of my love and fidelity. In the name
of the Father, and of the Son, and of the Holy Spirit.

The bride places her husband's ring on his ring finger. She may say:

N., take this ring as a sign of my love and fidelity. In the name of the Father, and of the Son, and of the Holy Spirit.

GENERAL INTERCESSIONS

The general intercessions (prayer of the faithful) follow. If the rubrics call for it, the profession of faith is said after the general intercessions.

PRAYER OVER THE GIFTS

Lord,
accept our offering for
this newly-married couple, N. and N.
By your love and providence you have brought them
    together;
now bless them all the days of their married life.
We ask this through Christ our Lord.

ALTERNATIVE PRAYERS

Lord,
accept the gifts we offer you
on this happy day.
In your fatherly love
watch over and protect N. and N.,
whom you have united in marriage.
We ask this through Christ our Lord.

or:

Lord,
hear our prayers
and accept the gifts we offer for N. and N.
Today you have made them one in the sacrament
    of marriage.
May the mystery of Christ's unselfish love,
which we celebrate in this eucharist,
increase their love for you and for each other.
We ask this through Christ our Lord.

LITURGY OF THE EUCHARIST

The Order of Mass is followed, with the following changes. During the preparation of the altar and gifts, the bride and bridegroom may bring the bread and wine to the altar.

PREFACE OF MARRIAGE I

Father, all-powerful and ever-living God,
we do well always and everywhere to give you thanks.

By this sacrament your grace unites man and woman
in an unbreakable bond of love and peace.

You have designed the chaste love of husband and wife
for the increase both of the human family
and of your own family born in baptism.

You are the loving Father of the world of nature;
you are the loving Father of the new creation of grace.
In Christian marriage you bring together the two orders
    of creation:
nature's gift of children enriches the world
and your grace enriches also your Church.

Through Christ the choirs of angels
and all the saints
praise and worship your glory.
May our voices blend with theirs
as we join in their unending hymn:

**Holy, holy, holy Lord, God of power and might,
heaven and earth are full of your glory.
    Hosanna in the highest,
Blessed is he who comes in the name of the Lord.
    Hosanna in the highest.**

PREFACE OF MARRIAGE II

Father, all-powerful and ever-living God,
we do well always and everywhere to give you thanks
through Jesus Christ our Lord.

Through him you entered into a new covenant
    with your people.
You restored man to grace
    in the saving mystery of redemption.

You gave him a share in the divine life
through his union with Christ.
You made him an heir of Christ's eternal glory.

This outpouring of love in the new covenant of grace
is symbolized in the marriage covenant
that seals the love of husband and wife
and reflects your divine plan of love.

And so, with the angels and all the saints in heaven
we proclaim your glory
and join in their unending hymn of praise:

**Holy, holy, holy Lord, God of power and might,
heaven and earth are full of your glory.**
    Hosanna in the highest,
Blessed is he who comes in the name of the Lord.
    Hosanna in the highest.

PREFACE OF MARRIAGE III

Father, all-powerful and ever-living God,
we do well always and everywhere to give you thanks.

You created man in love to share your divine life.
We see his high destiny in the love of husband and wife,
which bears the imprint of your own divine love.

Love is man's origin,
love is his constant calling,
love is his fulfillment in heaven.

The love of man and woman
is made holy in the sacrament of marriage,
 and becomes the mirror of your everlasting love.

Through Christ the choirs of angels
and all the saints
praise and worship your glory.
May our voices blend with theirs
as we join in their unending hymn:

**Holy, holy, holy Lord, God of power and might,
heaven and earth are full of your glory.**
    Hosanna in the highest,
Blessed is he who comes in the name of the Lord.
    Hosanna in the highest.

When Eucharistic Prayer I is used, the special form of Father, accept this offering is said. The words in brackets and parentheses may be omitted if desired.

Father, accept this offering
from your whole family
and from N. and N., for whom we now pray.
You have brought them to their wedding day:
grant them (the gift and joy of children and)
a long and happy life together.
[Through Christ our Lord. Amen.]

NUPTIAL BLESSING

After the Lord's Prayer, the prayer Deliver us is omitted. The priest faces the bride and bridegroom and says the following blessing over them.

If one or both of the parties will not be receiving communion, the words **through the sacrament of the body and blood of Christ**, may be omitted.

My dear friends, let us turn to the Lord and pray
that he will bless with his grace this woman (or N.)
now married in Christ to this man (or N.)
and that (through the sacrament of the body
    and blood of Christ,)
he will unite in love the couple he has joined
    in this holy bond.

All pray silently for a short while. Then the priest extends his hands and continues with the following prayer.

If desired two of the first three paragraphs may be omitted, keeping only the paragraph which corresponds to the reading the Mass.

Father,
by your power you have made everything out of nothing.
In the beginning you created the universe
and made mankind in your own likeness.
You gave man the constant help of woman
so that man and woman should no longer be two,
    but one flesh,
and you teach us that what you have united
may never be divided.

Father, you have made the union of man and wife so holy
    a mystery
that it symbolizes the marriage of Christ and his Church.

Father,
by your plan man and woman are united,
and married life has been established
as the one blessing that was not forfeited by original sin
or washed away in the flood.

Look with love upon this woman, your daughter,
now joined to her husband in marriage.
She asks your blessing.
Give her the grace of love and peace.
May she always follow the example of the holy women
whose praises are sung in the scriptures.

May her husband put his trust in her
and recognize that she is his equal
and the heir with him to the life of grace.
May he always honor her and love her
as Christ loves his bride, the Church.

Father,
keep them always true to your commandments.
Keep them faithful in marriage
and let them be living examples of Christian life.

Give them the strength which comes from the gospel
so that they may be witnesses of Christ to others.
(Bless them with children
and help them to be good parents.
(May they live to see their children's children.))

And, after a happy old age,
grant them fullness of life with the saints
in the kingdom of heaven.

We ask this through Christ our Lord.

R. Amen.

In the last paragraph of this prayer, the words in parentheses may be omitted whenever circumstances suggest it, for example, if the couple is advanced in years.

In the following prayer, either the paragraph **Holy Father, you created mankind**, or the paragraph **Father, to reveal the plan of your love**, may be omitted, keeping only the paragraph which corresponds to the reading of the Mass. The priest faces the bride and bridegroom and, with hands joined, says:

Let us pray to the Lord for N. and N.
who come to God's altar at the beginning
    of their married life
so that they may always be united in love for each other
(as now they share in the body and blood of Christ).

All pray silently for a short while. Then the priest extends his hands and continues:

Holy Father,
you created mankind in your own image
and made man and woman to be joined as husband
    and wife
in union of body and heart and so fulfill their mission
    in this world.
Father, to reveal the plan of your love,
you made the union of husband and wife
an image of the covenant between you and your people.
In the fulfillment of this sacrament,
the marriage of Christian man and woman
is a sign of the marriage between Christ and the Church.
Father, stretch out your hand, and bless N. and N.

Lord, grant that as they begin to live this sacrament
they may share with each other the gifts of your love
and become one in heart and mind
as witnesses to your presence in their marriage.
Help them to create a home together
(and give them children to be formed by the gospel
and to have a place in your family).
Give your blessings to N., your daughter,
so that she may be a good wife (and mother),
caring for the home,
faithful in love for her husband,
generous and kind.
Give your blessings to N., your son,
so that he may be a faithful husband
(and a good father).
Father, grant that as they come together to your table
    on earth,
so they may one day have the joy of sharing your feast
    in heaven.
We ask this through Christ our Lord.
R. Amen.

ALTERNATIVE NUPTIAL BLESSINGS

or:

The priest faces the bride and bridegroom and, with hands joined, says:

My dear friends, let us ask God
for his continued blessings upon this bridegroom
    and his bride (or N. and N.).

All pray silently for a short while. Then the priest extends his hands and continues:

Holy Father, creator of the universe,
maker of man and woman in your own likeness,
source of blessing for married life,
we humbly pray to you for this woman
who today is united with her husband
    in this sacrament of marriage.

May your fullest blessing come upon her and
    her husband
so that they may together rejoice in your gift
    of married love
(and enrich your Church with their children).

Lord, may they both praise you when they are happy
and turn to you in their sorrows.
May they be glad that you help them in their work
and know that you are with them in their need.
May they pray to you in the community of the Church,
and be your witnesses in the world.
May they reach old age in the company of their friends,
and come at last to the kingdom of heaven.

We ask this through Christ our Lord.

R. Amen.

SIGN OF PEACE

At the words Let us offer each other the sign of peace, the married couple and all present show their peace and love for one another in an appropriate way.

COMMUNION

The married couple may receive communion under both kinds.

(See Guidelines for Communion in page 147.)

PRAYER AFTER COMMUNION

Lord,
in your love
you have given us this eucharist
to unite us with one another and with you.
As you have made N. and N.
one in this sacrament of marriage
(and in the sharing of the one bread and the one cup,)
so now make them one in love for each other.
We ask this through Christ our Lord.

ALTERNATIVE PRAYERS

Lord,
we who have shared the food of your table
pray for our friends N. and N.,
whom you have joined together in marriage.
Keep them close to you always.
May their love for each other
proclaim to all the world
their faith in you.
We ask this through Christ our Lord.

or:

Almighty God,
may the sacrifice we have offered
and the eucharist we have shared
strengthen the love of N. and N.,
and give us all your fatherly aid.
We ask this through Christ our Lord.

SOLEMN BLESSING

Before blessing the people at the end of Mass, the priest blesses the bride and bridegroom, using one of the forms.

God the eternal Father keep you in love with each other,
so that the peace of Christ may stay with you
and be always in your home.
R. Amen.
May (your children bless you,)
your friends console you
and all men live in peace with you.
R. Amen.
May you always bear witness to the love of God in
    this world
so that the afflicted and the needy
will find in you generous friends
and welcome you into the joys of heaven.
R. Amen.
May almighty God bless you,
the Father, the Son, + and the Holy Spirit.
R. Amen.

A L T E R N A T I V E   B L E S S I N G S

May God, the almighty Father,
give you his joy
and bless you (in your children).
R. Amen.
May the only Son of God have mercy on you
and help you in good times and in bad.
R. Amen.
May the Holy Spirit of God
always fill your hearts with his love.
R. Amen.
And may almighty God bless you all,
the Father, and the Son, + and the Holy Spirit.
R. Amen.

or:

May the Lord Jesus, who was a guest at the wedding
    in Cana,
bless you and your families and friends.
R. Amen.
May Jesus, who loved his Church to the end,
always fill your hearts with his love.
R. Amen.

May he grant that, as you believe in his resurrection,
so you may wait for him in joy and hope.
R. Amen.
And may almighty God bless you all,
the Father, and the Son, + and the Holy Spirit.
R. Amen.

In the dioceses of the United States, the following form may be used:
May almighty God, with his Word of blessing,
unite your hearts in the never-ending bond of pure love.
R. Amen.
May your children bring you happiness,
and may your generous love for them be returned
to you,
many times over.
R. Amen.
May the peace of Christ live always in your hearts
and in your home.
May you have true friends to stand by you,
both in joy and in sorrow.
May you be ready and willing to help and comfort all
who come to you in need.
And may the blessings promised to the compassionate
be yours in abundance.
R. Amen.
May you find happiness and satisfaction in your work.
May daily problems never cause you undue anxiety,
nor the desire for earthly possessions dominate
your lives.
But may your hearts' first desire be always
the good things
waiting for you in the life of heaven.
R. Amen.
May the Lord bless you with many happy years together,
so that you may enjoy the rewards of a good life.
And after you have served him loyally in his kingdom
on earth,
may he welcome you to his eternal kingdom in heaven.
R. Amen.
And may almighty God bless you all,
the Father, and the Son, + and the Holy Spirit.
R. Amen..

F. GUIDELINES FOR RECEIVING COMMUNION

FOR CATHOLICS

Catholics fully participate in the celebration of the Eucharist when they receive Holy Communion in fulfillment of Christ's command to eat His Body and drink His Blood. In order to be properly disposed to receive Communion, communicants should not be conscious of grave sin, have fasted for one hour, and seek to live in charity and love with their neighbors. Persons conscious of grave sin must first be reconciled with God and the Church through the sacrament of Penance. A frequent reception of the sacrament of Penance is encouraged for all.

FOR OTHER CHRISTIANS

We welcome to this celebration of the Eucharist those Christians who are not fully united with us. It is a consequence of the sad divisions in Christianity that we cannot extend to them a general invitation to receive Communion. Catholics believe that the Eucharist is an action of the celebrating community signifying a oneness in faith, life, and worshipping of the community. Reception of the Eucharist by Christians not fully united with us would imply a oneness which does not yet exist, and for which we must all pray.

FOR THOSE NOT RECEIVING COMMUNION

Those not receiving sacramental Communion are encouraged to express in their hearts a prayerful desire for unity with the Lord Jesus and with one another.

FOR NON-CHRISTIANS

We also welcome to this celebration those who do not share our faith in Jesus. While we cannot extend to them an invitation to receive Communion, we do invite them to be united with us in prayer.

National Conference of Catholic Bishops

November 8, 1986 Washington, D.C.

G. RECOMMENDED BOOKS AND PERIODICALS

A. SUGGESTED READINGS FOR THOSE ENGAGED

- Abad, Javier & Fenoy, E. *Marriage: A path to sanctity.* Manila: Sinag-Tala Publishers Inc., 1988
- Escriva, Bl. Josemaria. *Marriage: A Christian Vocation.* Princeton: Scepter Publishers, 1970
- Kippley, John F. *Marriage is for Keeps. Foundations of Christian Marriage.* Cincinnati: The Foundation for the Family,1994.
- Smalley, Gary. *For Better or for Best: A valuable guide to knowing, understanding and loving your wife.* Grand Rapids: Zondervan, 1988.
- Smalley, Gary. *If only he knew: A valuable guide to knowing, understanding and loving your husband.* Grand Rapids: Zondervan, 1988.
- Burke, Rev. Cormac. *Covenanted Happiness.* San Francisco: Ignatius Press, 1990.
- Urteaga, J. *God and Children.* Princeton: Scepter Publishers, 1970
- Fightlin, Marshall. *A Catholic Understanding of Marital Intimacy.* Princeton: Scepter Publishers, 1976
- Chesterton, G. K. (edited by Alvaro de Silva). *Brave New Family.* San Francisco: Ignatius Press, 1990.
- Fallace, C. & J. *Sexual Affection in Marriage.* Lake Grove, NY: Little Flower Publications,1993

B. TEACHINGS OF THE CHURCH
(*all publications available in Daughters of St. Paul bookstores*)

- *Catechism of the Catholic Church*, Washington D. C.: U. S. Catholic Conference, 1994

- Pope John Paul II. *On the Role of the Family*. Rome: Libreria Editrice Vaticana, 1981
- Pope John Paul II. *On the Dignity and Vocation of Women*. Rome: Libreria Editrice Vaticana, 1988
- Pope John Paul II. *The Splendor of the Truth*. Rome: Libreria Editrice Vaticana, 1993
- Pope John Paul II. *Letter to Families*. Rome: Libreria Editrice Vaticana, 1994
- Pope Paul VI. *Humanae Vitae (On Human Life)*. Rome: Libreria Editrice Vaticana, 1968
- Congregation for Catholic Education. *Educational Guidance in Human Love*. Rome: Libreria Editrice Vaticana, 1975
- Congregation for the Doctrine of the Faith. *Declaration on Certain Questions of Sexual Ethics*. Rome: Libreria Editrice Vaticana, 1975
- Bishops' Committee for Pro-Life Activities, NCCB. *Natural Family Planning*. Washington D. C.: U. S. Catholic Conference, 1990
- Charter of the Rights of the Family. Washington D. C.: U. S. Catholic Conference, 1990

INDEX

188 *Marriage is Love Forever*